Agoraphobia

Agoraphobia

RUTH HURST VOSE

FABER AND FABER
London · Boston

First published in 1981
by Faber and Faber Limited
3 Queen Square London WC1N 3AU
Printed in Great Britain by
Willmer Brothers Limited, Rock Ferry, Merseyside
All rights reserved

British Library Cataloguing in Publication Data

Vose, Ruth Hurst
    Agoraphobia.
    1. Agoraphobia
    I. Title
    616.85'22   RC535

    ISBN 0-571-11752-X
    ISBN 0-571-11753-8 Pbk

Agoraphobia

RUTH HURST VOSE

FABER AND FABER
London · Boston

First published in 1981
by Faber and Faber Limited
3 Queen Square London WC1N 3AU
Printed in Great Britain by
Willmer Brothers Limited, Rock Ferry, Merseyside
All rights reserved

British Library Cataloguing in Publication Data

Vose, Ruth Hurst
  Agoraphobia.
  1. Agoraphobia
  I. Title
  616.85'22   RC535

  ISBN 0-571-11752-X
  ISBN 0-571-11753-8 Pbk

To James Edward

Contents

Author's Note

My attempt at walking the delicate line between technical accuracy and readability has meant that I have grouped most of the
statistics and articles concerning agoraphobia in an appendix and
select bibliography at the end of the book. Nevertheless some
articles could not be totally ignored within the main text and are
listed at the end of each chapter. The chapters on the various treatments are inevitably a little more complicated but I have tried to
keep medical terminology at a level acceptable to both the medical
person and the ordinary reader. Addresses useful to both agoraphobes and their doctors and therapists are listed in a further
appendix.

Acknowledgements

My sincerest thanks go to those named in the book who gave me information and to the many agoraphobes who wished to remain anonymous while providing much illuminating material.

Special thanks go to Mona Woodford, National Organiser of The Open Door Association, for her help and work in surveying her members, and to Katherine Fisher, President of The Phobics Society, for her advice and support. John Convey, Computerised Information Retrieval Services Librarian for Lancashire, produced a large and regular supply of phobia references and Jean Perkins, Assistant Librarian at Edge Hill College of Higher Education, helped me trace the more obscure items. Faber and Faber Inc. found some valuable American references and addresses.

A press cuttings search was organised by Ian Fletcher, *Daily Mail* Staff Reporter, with the cooperation of the *Daily Mail* Cuttings Library, and Eileen Fletcher gave generous help in gathering information on spiritual healing.

I am indebted to Peter Blythe of the Chester Institute for Neuro-Physiological Psychology for clarifying the mysteries of organic brain dysfunction and improving my technical accuracy.

My best thanks go to my husband Jim for his comments, advice and unbounded enthusiasm for the book.

Maureen Charsley typed the manuscript.

My apologies go to those who sent me information which owing to limitations of space I have been unable to use.

R.H.V.

Chapter 1

The Onset of Agoraphobia

The American Airlines Boeing 727 from New York's Kennedy airport dropped through the darkness ready for a smooth landing at Boston airport. Weary passengers filed out of the plane and tramped through the dirty corridors of the huge airport to their various destinations. Among them were an English farmer and his wife. She had completed the first fortnight of a gruelling lecture tour of the United States of America and Canada. She was about to experience her first bout of agoraphobia, which is where my story begins.

There hadn't been much of a break for me between directing a backbreaking archaeological excavation in a river valley near Manchester in England, and the three weeks' lecture tour. A 12-hour working day for seven days a week had been the pattern of the excavation, with television, radio and newspaper interviews to cope with on a nationally important site.

Little time had been available to put together the lectures I was to give as guest speaker at American and Canadian museums and institutions. Luckily my programme in New York, Toledo and Virginia had gone well, but at Boston the airport handed out the straw which broke the camel's back. Our cases were lost, including the only slides existing of the season's excavations, which is a true lecturer's nightmare.

'I was so tired and mixed up, I started a tendency which continued to call people and places by completely the wrong names,' I wrote on that day's travel notes.

Slight stomach pains started during the next day's crowded programme and after eating at Boston's famous Market Place Inn in the evening, retribution for four years' overwork and 15 days' non-stop travelling set in. My body and mind seized up. I could neither move nor think.

That night I talked to my husband Jim about the possibility of having to go home—though the prospect of such a long journey was almost as bad as carrying on to Ottawa. With my whole being screaming to be at rest at home I hugged a pillow to my stomach and hoped for the best.

The Boston seize-up was not agoraphobia in the true sense, but it signalled the onset of symptoms which eventually made me a prisoner in my own home. Our luggage was in fact relocated and I completed the tour, which had involved 21 air flights in as many days.

It was about this time that Jim and I decided to take a winter vacation in Torremolinos, which was just beginning its development as a major Spanish tourist centre. This was to be a special holiday, the first time since we got married that we had been abroad with no lectures or work involved. The holiday began as a real tonic, and being typical tourists we decided to take a coach trip to Granada to see the Alhambra, the 13th-century Arabic palace of great beauty just outside the city. We got seats at the back of the coach but suddenly, just as the coach set off, I knew I had to get out.

Fearful and sweaty, I just wanted to get off and be in the fresh air outside, or better still, back at the hotel. To make matters worse, the sudden tension made me want to go to the lavatory but the coach was not due to make a stop for two hours. Too proud and ashamed to dash to the front of the coach and ask the driver to stop, a nightmare journey followed.

On arrival at Granada, there were no problems looking round the large and amazingly cool cathedral, and walking round the beautiful Alhambra, part of which was indeed a gilded cage for the women of the harem so long ago. The prospect of the journey back was almost unthinkable, but it had to be faced since there was no way out. Thoroughly terrified, I forced myself to chat to a lady in the seat next to me to take my mind off the journey, an approach which worked to some extent, but coach journeys for the future became an impossibility. Oddly, flying back home after the holiday presented no problems, and I pushed the incident out of my mind.

Back once more at work, I received an invitation to give a paper at a conference in Wiesbaden, Germany. For no reason at all, I knew I couldn't go. Fortunately another person was available to take my place, so any personal crisis was averted for the time being.

The next link in the chain came with a lecture trip to a Welsh university. I stopped at a cafe for a quick snack half-way through the car journey, then things began to go badly wrong. All the apparent symptoms of gastro-enteritis began to manifest themselves and there was no choice but to dash to the nearest toilet every ten minutes for the rest of the way. Badly shaken and humiliated, and terribly fearful of being unable to keep control of my stomach, I arrived at my destination, and the symptoms disappeared as suddenly as they came.

That was the first time my body had physically let me down, and it terrified me a great deal. I consciously believed I had eaten something at the cafe on the journey down which had given me an upset stomach, but a warning voice at the back of my mind told me it was something much more serious, which I certainly did not want to contemplate.

In the course of my job I made regular trips from Lancashire to London and enjoyed the train journey and meeting people very much. Once again a white wall of unreasoning panic gradually arose at the mere threat of having business in London, and I eventually refused to go.

By the summer of 1972 I was manifesting all the symptoms of a nervous wreck. Unable to sleep properly, with constant stomach pains, I lost a lot of weight and found it increasingly difficult to work. I insisted there had to be a physical cause, but my doctor assured me the extreme nausea, weakness and pain were due to an anxiety state. The fear that I was going 'nuts' which had been kept well to the back of my mind was immediately pushed to the fore. Although I took mild sedatives on the doctor's advice, I refused heavy drugs since I privately equated these with insanity.

The vicious spiral of events continued unabated until the fateful and decisive day when I was unable to get to work, a drive of about 15 miles. Crying and incoherent, I fled to the refuge of a friend's house half-way there, scared to death, confused and totally demoralised. I resigned from my job rather than face heavy drugs and psychiatric treatment.

With self-respect and self-confidence completely shattered, and no job to force me out of the house, my home closed in on me. I was more trapped than the poor women who had been incarcerated in Spain's Alhambra palace, with far less chance of escape.

Since I claim no uniqueness for my experience, perhaps a few more true life stories of how agoraphobia can creep up on anyone, regardless of class, intelligence, environment or anything else, are necessary.

A Gloucestershire man who had suffered from agoraphobia for nearly 50 years told me:

'I can best explain what I mean by agoraphobia by describing my first recognisable attack. Looking back into childhood, I can remember certain incidents which might have been phobic in nature rather than purely "physical" as I then thought; but the first certain attack was one pleasant day when I was 17. I had an appointment with the family dentist—a nice chap of whom I had no fear, and so far as I remember the visit portended no horrors, though dentistry then was not the almost pleasant encounter it is today.

'I decided to walk, the distance being perhaps a couple of miles, which meant nothing to me in those days. I had got perhaps a quarter of a mile, and was passing some suburban shops when I was suddenly struck with an overwhelming feeling of faintness, but above all of impending doom: an irresistible panic which made it essential that I turn and struggle *back home*—legs weak and useless, apparently unable to carry me; heart pounding wildly, say 140 plus; a tendency for the world to look dark, and above all distant and unreal. As I got nearer to home, the fear subsided. Once back there, I could not understand what had happened to me.

Without being too dramatic, I can say with simple truth that my life has never been the same again.'

A Somerset housewife and mother of two boys had her first and very bad attack of panic when she was 13 years old on her way to school. She explains:

'At the time neither my parents, doctor or I had any idea what it was, but our doctor was very helpful and put us in touch with the right people. I ended up at the Maudsley Hospital in London. They were wonderful and after approximately nine months as a patient, I was 95 per cent cured.

'By this time I was 17 years old and started to live a normal life again. Almost, that is, as I did not like walking over bridges or going up very tall buildings or walking along the sea front, but these were things I could easily avoid.

'It all started coming back about 10 years ago after we came here to live. Having had a successful career in London, I was unable to get work here and that led to me being indoors all day long, in a strange town etc. One thing led to another and after the birth of our youngest child I was completely housebound—could not even go into the garden to hang up the washing.'

Stress of all kinds has a big part to play in triggering off agoraphobic symptoms, as I found to my own cost. It does not have to be 'unpleasant' stress either. 'Pleasant' stress can be just as lethal, such as the joy and upset of having a baby, or the excitement of a lecture tour.

A mother of eight children from Northern Ireland described for me the onset of her agoraphobia, after the birth of her first child. Her own childhood had been very upset by the death of her mother, resulting in her and her brothers and sisters having to be put in homes. When she was 19 years old and trained as a children's nurse, she became pregnant, which delighted her and her boyfriend.

'To get pregnant then in our town was terrible, so we were sent off to England, where we got married. We could not get accom-

modation, so we had to come back again. Then the trouble started.
I had the baby at my mother-in-law's house. It was an easy birth,
but I lost a lot of blood as the afterbirth did not all come away at
once.

'When baby was two weeks old I took her for a walk and took a
dizzy turn going along the street. I went back home and was afraid
all evening. My mother-in-law thought I was a lazy good-for-
nothing person because I was afraid to get up off the chair or do
anything in case my heart started thumping, or I got dizzy.'

During the next eight years, she had her eight children and
suffered irregularly from panic symptoms, although always managing to cope. With the marriage of her two eldest daughters she
was sometimes free of her symptoms for months at a time.

'Then one evening I was walking into town to do a friend's hair,
when I got dizzy. I came home, heart pounding, sweating, etc. The
next day I felt seasick when I walked, but okay when I sat down.
And that was the start. I was practically housebound, could not
go out into the garden to hang up washing, bring in coal and I
had to have my bread and groceries delivered to my house.'

A 24-year-old London woman described her run-up to true agoraphobia, which gradually took over during a period of 11 years.

'My first experience was at about the age of eight. My mother
had taken me to see the doctor, and on the way home from the
surgery I was, unfortunately, sick in the street, and my mother
reprimanded me severely, told me how dirty I was and walked
away from me refusing to walk along the street with me.'

When she was 13 years old her father died after a long illness,
which left her totally bewildered. She was not allowed to go to his
cremation and to this day does not know where her father's ashes
are laid. She became ill and two months later a serious kidney
disease was diagnosed. She was very nervous and refused to go out
unaccompanied.

'When I was 15, agoraphobia had set in, although I was still
blaming my kidney disease. I would go out with my mother, and
as soon as I went into a building I would panic, and would sud-

denly be all right again when out of the situation. At 18, desperate
to break away from a domineering mother and an unhappy home,
with the constant anxiety of trying to keep going into work, I
decided that the best way out was to have a baby, so I did. [Living
with her boyfriend.] I had a girl amid total anxiety at the state of
my health, and that is when agoraphobia really started.'

The stress of severe sickness and operations can often act as the
trigger for agoraphobia. A Welsh lady had a gall bladder operation,
and recovered very quickly. Six weeks after the operation she was
playing volley-ball in her back garden.

'I don't remember how long after it was, but I began to get un-
easy, as if I was about to be ill standing at bus stops. I remember
collecting one of my children from school to take her to the dentist,
and while we were waiting at the bus stop, suddenly becoming
terrified that I was going to be ill. I felt my bowels liquefying, and
remember frantically trying to calculate if I could get across the
road to the public toilets before the bus came. The bus arrived and
I sat on the long seat so that I could jump off quickly if . . . what?
I didn't actually want to be sick or go to the lavatory but I was
sure that something awful was going to happen and I would have
to get off the bus. I made it to the dentist all right without getting
off, but it was pretty dreadful.'

Because the last thing agoraphobes want is for anyone to know of
their disability, biographies and autobiographies of sufferers are
comparatively rare. Of those which have been written, the motivation of the writers seems to be a compelling urge to throw (they
hope) some light on the problem by recounting their own experiences. If an agoraphobia sufferer has managed to achieve a cure,
his natural reaction is to forget the pain belonging to the past, and
get back to normality as quickly as possible. Hence books written
by agoraphobes who have got better are very rare indeed.

The desire for anonymity is retained by 'David', who persuaded
Ernest Raymond to edit a mass of autobiographical detail on his

sufferings, which was published in 1946. The result is a moving and fascinating publication, revealing how, against almost insuperable agoraphobic odds, David rose to be a top Fleet Street journalist.

Like many agoraphobes, David shared an intense desire to give sense and purpose to his agony, since one almost feels that—unless the whole world is mad—such suffering has to have a purpose. 'For this I was brought into the world: this I have done' was a possible title David had in mind when he was disciplining himself to put together his autobiographical notes, dedicating the book to 'my friends the insane; to all those who have known the dark way towards the light ... to those who are seeking to understand the mysterious forces which control human behaviour; to those who believe in a divine purpose behind apparent chaos ...' Although his autobiography was almost the last thing he wished to write, he felt he had to as 'a gesture of faith in the Universe'.

David longed to see that what had happened to him should be of help to others, especially to the helplessly insane who could not speak for themselves. He had harrowing experience of mental homes and asylums, and besides his fear of open spaces, he also had a compulsion to self-exposure. His description of the latter habit, repulsive though it is to ordinary people, gives an insight into the totally overwhelming forces behind it, moving the censorious to a rather helpless sympathy.

A tall, handsome, stylish man, David found a stronghold in Fleet Street despite his dreadful disabilities, becoming London Editor of the Scottish *Daily Record* and *Sunday Mail*. His fight against agoraphobia which he fled from and fought for over 40 years reaches almost epic proportions, with success almost within grasp before his final fall into an almost completely housebound state.

A courageous and most sensitive person, he was acquainted with many famous names of his time including Bonar Law and Ramsay MacDonald, and Shaw, Wells and Bennett. He kept his malady concealed out of a sense of shame, turning from the subject with loathing when he was feeling healthier.

David retained his anonymity, as did 'Vincent', who wrote his

'Confessions of an Agoraphobic Victim' in 1919. An American, Vincent was middle-aged when he wrote the article, and admitted to having agoraphobia since the age of 12. Like David, Vincent was by no means a nonentity. He describes himself as a person of leadership in his town and a public speaker of ability. No one knew of his condition, or apparently suspected him of having agoraphobia. Vincent felt the same commitment to describe his strange illness, which had never left him for a minute since his first encounter. The paramount question for Vincent was whether there was hope of a cure, so that people like him could at last be like other men, taking their normal place in society.

Another American, Professor William Ellery Leonard, taught English at the University of Wisconsin and published many books and articles, including an extraordinary account of his unsuccessful fight against years of agoraphobia, published in 1928. His motive in embarking on what was to be a two years' intensive study of his condition was twofold: to produce a valuable scientific document, added to the hope of finding a cure. At the age of 50 he had suffered extreme agoraphobia for 15 years, but his minute research resulted in complete failure to find a cure. He admits this, but hopes that someone will find value in his case.

Reflecting on the sometimes harsh treatment he received from outsiders, he adds: 'One purpose of this book is to make normal people—neighbours, friends, pastors, doctors—safer for the thousands of other phobiacs in the world today or tomorrow.'

Of the few accounts of agoraphobes who write of their recovery, Mrs F. H. (still retaining her anonymity) shows courage and ingenuity in her self-help and analysis on a long road to recovery. Badly photophobic (afraid of light), she had her first panic at the age of 25, and records her eventual full recovery 30 years later. In her autobiographical notes (Anon, 1952), she says she had no wish to dwell on her sufferings, but wanted to present an accurate picture of someone who was subject to overwhelming fears over such a long stretch of time, and who recovered completely—indeed a triumph of hope over immense odds.

Perhaps it is a sign that agoraphobia is becoming slightly more socially acceptable that two former agoraphobia sufferers have published their stories without any attempt at anonymity in recent years: David Lazell (1973) tells how he came to cope with his agoraphobia, and Stanley N. Law (1975) tells his story of ultimate success.

Since most agoraphobic and ex-agoraphobic authors hope their sufferings will be enlightening to others, it is worth recounting some of their more important or decisive experiences. The onset of agoraphobia for those publicly moved to set down their life histories is as different (and similar) as it is for the hundred of thousands who prefer to keep their torment to themselves.

Childhood memories for the journalist David were not happy. His mother died when he was very young, and his childhood was dominated by his father, a puritanically religious man who administered sound thrashings for the transgressions of his large and poor family. Against this unpromising background, David had his first brief encounter with his life's enemy on the lovely slopes of Ben Vahren in Scotland. Half-way up the mountain, he was suddenly overcome by the immense scenery, feeling lost and a minute particle without any place in the menacing universe. He started to run in panic from he knew not what, and had to run for some time before the overwhelming feelings left him.

When David left school, his first job was in a wholesale warehouse which he loathed. He became more and more miserable, and it was at this time that the first signs of acute nervousness began to make their appearance. He had been sent on a message by his employers, and as he got off the tram in which he was travelling, he suddenly felt he dared not move. 'A strange fear seized me, I gasped for breath, and my heart beat violently,' he described. After sitting in a nearby shop, David's attack passed off, but two weeks later he got a sore throat and 'nervous prostration' set in, putting him in bed for weeks. Because of this it was decided that he should no longer work at the warehouse, and his symptoms disappeared for the time being (Raymond, 1946).

His experience is an excellent example of one of the undoubted advantages of agoraphobia. It can provide unconsciously a most convenient escape from life's problems. In this case, David's symptoms clearly paid off, getting him out of a situation he heartily disliked.

Nervous and introspective as a child, Vincent started showing symptoms of agoraphobia following a local tragedy when a boy was found murdered, which depressed him a great deal. While coasting down a high hill not far from his country home with some other boys, he experienced an uncomfortable feeling every time they returned to the top of the hill. The symptoms developed over the next few months, with the result that he avoided hill-tops as far as possible. Within a year his fears had expanded to take in wide fields, high things, crowds of people and, later, wide streets and parks.

One has to read nearly 300 pages of Professor Leonard's exhaustive and difficult account before reaching his first full-blooded attack of agoraphobia. It happened seven miles from home on a walk with a friend to West Point at the lower end of Lake Mendota. Calling it the most significant moment in his entire book, the description occupies several pages, but the following sentences serve to illustrate the severity of the attack.

'I am convinced this is my last hour ... perhaps my last minute ... I am all the while mad with the terror and despair of being so far from home and parents ... I am alone, alone, in the universe ... I am running round and round in a circle shrieking, when Charlie emerges from the woods ... I have another seizure.'

He offers the owners of a vehicle standing nearby any payment to get him back to town at once, and the young people accept. 'They drive fast. I breathe deep, holding myself together. Counting the landmarks, mile by mile. We get out at the Cottage. I shake with terror ... I guess I am dying.'

When he wakes the next morning, Professor Leonard attempts

to go for a walk. Within 100 feet of the house he is compelled to rush back in horror of being so far away from home and security. 'I have never walked or ridden, alone or with others, as a normal man since that day,' he concludes (Leonard, 1928).

Stanley Law's first attack, which occurred a few decades later than Ellery Leonard's experience, is equally as harrowing, with Law actually collapsing in the street, gasping for air, feeling death was imminent. (As most agoraphobes fear collapsing in just such a situation, it is worth pointing out that the only practical result at the time was that a passer-by helped Law to get up, and he returned home to his wife.)

In contrast, David Lazell's agoraphobia was not quite so incapacitating. He had his first attack in his middle teens, but it took another 25 years before he reached the stage where he was no longer able to cope with leading a normal life. Before he finally went for treatment he was a senior salesman in a hi-fi store, but could only get to work if his wife accompanied him. Quite frequently he might order a meal in a restaurant and leave it untouched because of an attack of panic.

Every agoraphobe has a different tale to tell of how it all started, but the similarities are there. The overwhelming nature of the panic is shared by everyone in varying intensities from shrieking panic to a breathless stillness. Another common factor is the feeling of complete bewilderment over the initial and subsequent attacks. Certainly the victim has no idea why it is happening, and could be forgiven for putting an entirely religious significance on it, since the attack comes like an avenging demon out of the blue. More often than not, the family doctor also has no idea where the attacks are coming from, which offers little comfort to someone who was leading an apparently normal life and has suddenly become completely incapacitated by fear. In all the literature written by and about agoraphobes, the central questions of 'Why me?' or

'Why?' at all, have never been satisfactorily answered.

This book endeavours to answer both queries in full, making sense of the sufferings of millions through the centuries and especially in modern stress-ridden society.

REFERENCES

(Anon) F. H. (Mrs) (1952). Recovery from a Long Neurosis. *Psychiatry*, 15, 161–177.

(Anon) Vincent (1919). Confessions of an Agoraphobic Victim. *American Journal of Psychology*, 30, 295–299.

Law, Stanley N. (1975). *Inspired Freedom. Agoraphobia: A Battle Won.* Regency Press, London.

Lazell, David (1973). *I Couldn't Catch the Bus To-day. The True Story of a Nervous Breakdown that became a Pilgrimage.* Lutterworth Press, Guildford and London.

Leonard, William E. (1928). *The Locomotive God*, pp. 300–8. Chapman & Hall, London.

Raymond, Ernest (editor) (1946). *The Autobiography of David*, p. 44. Victor Gollancz, London.

Chapter 2

What is Agoraphobia?

A common and understandable misconception among agoraphobia sufferers is the feeling that you are the only person in the world suffering from this mystifying condition. Certainly I did not realise that I was an agoraphobe until at least six months after I finally succumbed to being housebound. If I had heard of the term, it was only in association with a vague image of old people refusing to leave their homes through some eccentricity. I did not associate it with the horrors of my own condition, which I thought was entirely unique.

In a sense I was right, since no two agoraphobes are ever quite the same. However, in another sense I was overwhelmingly wrong, since the latest conservative estimate of the number of agoraphobes in the United Kingdom is half a million. Most people involved in the treatment of agoraphobia agree that the number is likely to be much higher, since many (like myself) do not realise they are suffering from it, refuse to recognise it or admit that they have it since the prospect is too frightening, or are too afraid to go for treatment. Since agoraphobia is such a mixture of other anxiety neuroses, there is also a strong possibility of varying diagnosis, which adds more confusion to the possible statistics.

More importantly, I have no hesitation in stating that it is a very rare person indeed who has not at some time suffered slightly from agoraphobic symptoms. The majority of people do suffer from mild agoraphobia, providing fertile ground for the increase in true agoraphobes—those who can no longer cope or lead any semblance of a normal life due to their symptoms.

FEARS AND PHOBIAS

There is a great difference between ordinary or natural fear and a phobia, a fact not always easily apparent to a person who has never been involved with a phobia.

Fear is not a pleasant experience, but it is useful in that it will activate the 'flight or fight' mechanism which is necessary for survival in animals and humans. There is nothing unnatural and everything to gain from a healthy fear of dangerous or threatening situations, which has helped many a soldier to survive in battle, or a pedestrian to cross a busy street.

When fear is transferred to a particular object or situation, it becomes a phobia. A phobia is a special kind of fear, where the person knows that the object of his fear is not harmful, but cannot help the overwhelming feelings of terror which occur when he meets it. For example, women especially have a loathing for spiders (arachnophobia) out of all proportion to any harm the creatures could possibly inflict. No amount of reasoning or reassurance can persuade an arachnophobe to go near the eight-legged insect. The fear is apparently beyond voluntary control, and the person will do anything to avoid the feared situation again.

The new *Gould Medical Dictionary* classifies more than 275 phobias by name, and there are still more as yet unlisted. Apart from agoraphobia, it has been estimated that a minimum of four million people in the United Kingdom suffer from some form of phobic anxiety. The types of phobic disorders reported by 463 readers of the British weekly magazine *Woman* in 1976 showed nearly 50 per cent suffered from agoraphobia, the rest reporting fears in the following descending order of 'popularity': social situations, thunder and lightning, animals, disease (germs, contamination, dirt), being sick, travel, claustrophobia, being alone, lack of bladder/bowel control, dying, public speaking and heights. Fear of the dentist and miscellaneous fears, such as of the dark, having injections, loud noises and swallowing pills, came bottom of the list with less than four per cent (Burns and Thorpe, 1977a). This survey indicates, as do other surveys, that agoraphobia and, to a lesser extent, social phobia (15.31 per cent in the *Woman* survey) are the two major problem areas for phobic disorders in the western world.

Although an agoraphobe might look upon someone suffering from arachnophobia or any other phobia as being fairly fortunate, one should not underestimate the disruption specific phobias can wreak on sufferers' lives. One has only to imagine the problems of coping with such fears as eating in public, a fear of handling anything connected with animal fats, a fear of sleeping or even a fear of feathers or leaves. A Lancashire woman had an acute fear of sweet-papers which severely incapacitated her for over eight years. As long as the specific phobia sufferer can avoid the cause of the fear (dogs, cats, thunder, etc.) he/she can function reasonably normally and get on with life. An agoraphobia sufferer cannot do that, since the major fear is of going out. It is this which makes agoraphobia the most severe and handicapping of all the phobias, and one of the most difficult to cure.

DEFINITION

Before launching into a full description of what agoraphobia entails, it is worth examining the evolution and interpretation of the word itself. 'Agoraphobia' is an ugly-sounding word, possibly because of its modern connotations with the colloquialism 'aggro', and it has been criticised for failing to describe accurately the condition.

Agoraphobia can present such a miscellany of other phobic disorders and non-phobic symptoms that its existence as a clinical entity has been brought into question from time to time. Professor Isaac Marks of London's Institute of Psychiatry, and a leading phobia expert, points out that the most constant feature in the constellation of clinical events is a central core of phobias relating to the fear of public places, which does set it apart from other conditions. The term is used to describe conditions ranging from some travel phobias and claustrophobias where the term is over-inclusive and possibly misleading, to severe cases which include other phobias, depression, obsessions and other symptoms, where the term is under-inclusive and describes only a part of the whole clinical picture. Marks concludes that from clinical and statistical evidence, agoraphobia can be considered a coherent clinical syndrome with a well-defined cluster of features which carry on for long periods (Marks, 1969). There is no apparent continuity between the symptoms of an agoraphobe and the specific phobia sufferer, which again points to it being a clinical entity in its own right. Other research has suggested that agoraphobia should not be classified with phobias at all but should be seen as a variable feature of patients suffering from anxiety neurosis (Hallam, 1978).

Agoraphobia is derived from the Greek word *'agora'* meaning market place, assembly, or the place of assembly, and 'phobia', from the Greek word *'phobos'* meaning terror and flight. It has been suggested that it could now be updated to 'super-agoraphobia', or fear of the supermarket, due to a common modern agoraphobic problem. The word is often misinterpreted to mean 'fear of open spaces', which is both semantically and clinically incorrect. The term was first coined to cover fear of public places of assembly, which fits the central clinical facts.

The first person to use the term 'agoraphobia' was C. Westphal, a German psychiatrist, who wrote in 1871 of 'the impossibility of walking through certain streets or squares, or possibility of so doing only with resultant dread of anxiety'. Because the fear of going out is one of the major aspects of agoraphobia, the name has stuck, even though the fear of public places scarcely covers the huge variety of agoraphobic manifestations. Other names have been given by psychiatrists, none of which quite hits the nail fully on the head: phobic anxiety state, locomotor anxiety, topophobia, kenophobia, depersonalisation-phobic-anxiety-syndrome, anxiety hysteria, street fear, severe mixed psychoneurosis, pseudo-neurotic schizophrenia, and non-specific insecurity fears. One imagines that agoraphobia has retained its popularity as a name, since it appears to be the easiest to remember! The German term *'Platzangst'* and the French *'peur des espaces'* or *'horreur du vide'* have the same literal meaning as agoraphobia.

A common difficulty of agoraphobes is the inability to tolerate confinement in a hairdresser's, barber's or dentist's chair, since the way of immediate escape is blocked. This has earned its own name, being called 'the barber's chair syndrome' (Erwin, 1963). Erwin contended that physical or conditioned confinement is usually necessary, but not sufficient, for the production of human neuroses.

HISTORY

The term agoraphobia was first used just over a century ago, but the particular set of symptoms it covers has existed for thousands of years.

Hippocrates, the father of modern medicine, who lived between the fifth and fourth centuries BC, successfully treated the King of Macedon for melancholia, which shows that depression is not something confined to the 20th century. He is quoted in his writings describing someone who 'through bashfulness, suspicion, and timourousness, will not be seen abroad, loves darkness as life and cannot endure the light or to sit in lightsome places; his hat still in his eyes, he will neither see, nor be seen by his good will. He dare not come in company for fear he should be misused, disgraced, overshoot himself in gesture or speeches, or be sick; he thinks every man observes him ...' Not precisely agoraphobia, but definitely a near cousin.

History, literature and legend can provide examples of people who suffered from symptoms akin to agoraphobia. Augustus Caesar (27 BC–AD 14), one of the greatest Roman emperors, was at times plagued with nervous illness. Robert Burton, who wrote *Anatomy of Melancholy* in 1621, claimed that Augustus could not bear to sit in the dark. The Byzantine emperor Heraclius had a phobia of looking at the sea. Burton mentioned 'one that durst not walk alone from home, for fear he should swoon, or die ... If he be locked in a close room, he is afraid of being stifled for want of air, and still carries bisket aquavite, or some strong waters about him, for fear of deliquiums, or being sick; or if he be in a throng, middle of a church, multitude, where he may not well go out, though he sit at ease, he is so misaffected.'

Pascal, a contemporary of Descartes, apparently suffered from agoraphobia. The 19th-century Italian writer Manzoni was afraid of leaving the house, and especially of fainting while he was out, so carried a small bottle of concentrated vinegar wherever he went. The Cambridge philosopher McTaggart could never walk straight across an open space but had to sidle along, keeping his back to the wall. After Prince Albert's death, Queen Victoria became a virtual recluse, refusing to be seen in public for years. Charles Dickens's Miss Haversham, in *Great Expectations*, comes close to being an agoraphobe, remaining in her house surrounded by the remains of her happier past years after she was jilted. Millionaires like Howard Hughes can become virtual recluses in their own gilded cages, not far removed from the self-made trap of the agoraphobe. Even Sigmund Freud, the father of psychoanalysis, had a fear of travelling by train for a dozen years, and later on became so anxious that he sometimes arrived at the station an hour before the train was due. Agoraphobia sufferers have no need to feel they are alone in the world—in fact they have far too much company.

For the millions suffering from agoraphobia, and for those attempting to treat their condition, statistics on agoraphobia do not give much confidence that the battle against the rising tide of unnatural and terribly disabling fears is even beginning to be won. (See p. 184.) It would appear that the most people can hope for is that they can learn to cope with the fears and panic and lead some form of a 'normal' life, sometimes to the point of cure, or that the fears will sometimes mysteriously regress on their own.

Although agoraphobia has been dissected and examined from all points of view, it still retains its ultimate mystery. Researchers' and doctors' work in agoraphobia is so often punctuated with 'don't knows', 'unknown', and 'not understood'.

As stated earlier, the problem is everyone's heritage, since few of us have not had mild agoraphobic symptoms at some point in life. Before an important event, most people have a few butterflies in their stomachs, and even find walking into the full glare of a dance hall or restaurant rather difficult, feeling that all eyes are staring at them. In the theatre or cinema, there are quite a few of us who prefer to sit on the end of a row of seats to 'stretch our legs'. There are still many people who have never travelled abroad, or even been out of their own county or town, and they would never label themselves as having agoraphobia. Others rarely move outside the confines of their own family and tight circle of friends, blocking off the rest of the world by simply ignoring it. Not agoraphobia, but still a policy of fear.

Women and men who only feel comfortable taking the same route to work or to the shops, who are afraid to detour into unknown side streets, who feel a bit faint in the bustle of the town, who like to be near the door of the bus or the church, are not agoraphobes, but are living in a state of latent fear.

Men who like to keep to a strict routine: work and evening at home during the week, pub on Fridays, out with the wife on Saturdays, wash the car on Sundays, holidays in the same place every year—perhaps their life is a little too 'safe'.

Many of us feel embarrassed if our stomachs rumble in company, and feel slightly conspicuous going to the lavatory in a public house or any other public situation, sometimes even in a friend's house. Again, not agoraphobia, but very unnecessary feelings, and a definite shadow of the fear of loss of control which overhangs so many agoraphobes' lives.

I am certainly not implying that we live in a land of agoraphobia. A person only becomes an agoraphobe when he or she can no longer cope or lead a normal life any longer, because of mounting fears and panic. However, we do live in a land of potential agoraphobes, and there are a good 500 000 in the United Kingdom alone who have already crossed the borderline of coping. It is finding out what pushes that half million across that delicate borderline which is the problem, and wherein lies the answer to agoraphobia.

REFERENCES

Burns, L. E. and Thorpe, G. L. (1977a). Fears and Clinical Phobias: Epidemiological Aspects and the National Survey of Agoraphobics. *Journal of International Medical Research*, 5 (1), 134.

Erwin, W. J. (1963). Confinement in the Production of Human Neuroses: The Barber's Chair Syndrome. *Behavior Research and Therapy*, 1, 175–163.

Hallam, R. S. (1978). Agoraphobia: a Critical Review of the Concept. *British Journal of Psychiatry*, 133, 314–319.

Hippocrates. On Epidemics, V, Section LXXXII.

Marks, Isaac M. (1969). *Fears and Phobias*, p. 112. William Heinemann Medical Books, London.

Westphal, C. (1871–2). Die Agoraphobie: Eine Neuropathische Erscheinung. *Archiv für Psychiatrie und Nervenkrankheiten*, 3, 138–171, 219–221.

Chapter 3

The Terror

'So you would like to know what it's like to suffer from agoraphobia. One word can explain it—Hell!' a Welsh agoraphobe told me with vehemence. As hell is defined as a state of supreme misery or discomfort, or anything causing misery, pain or destruction, this would appear to be fair comment.

When I first considered writing this book, Jim said: 'You must get over to them exactly what it's like. Tell them that for you to go outside the door was like asking a man to jump from the top of a multi-storey building, except worse, because you were faced with it every minute of every day.' A very good point, and I was fortunate indeed to have someone who appreciated and accepted the extremes of terror to which I was subjected.

I compare the fear of the agoraphobe to the fear of the men in the trenches during the First World War, who were ordered to go 'over the top' in the full knowledge that they were almost certain to be killed. If you can just imagine for one moment the almost blind terror of many of those men, then you have felt a faint shadow of what agoraphobia is all about. That is what it feels like from the moment the severe agoraphobe wakes up to the moment he goes to sleep, and the fear often follows him into his dreams as well.

Vincent shared my view exactly. He had such a dread of walking across a long bridge that he reckoned it was easier for him to face a nest of Boche machine guns than walk to a part of his town across the river.

Professor Ellery Leonard wrote most compellingly on this point. He likened a trip by rail and boat to Boston and Fall River in the 1920s as exactly as unthinkable as a walk along a steel girder 35 storeys in the air on lower Broadway, or an aeroplane ride to the Pole. Describing the clearly defined degrees of emotional intensity in his agoraphobia, Leonard said:

'Let me assume that I am walking down University Drive by the Lake. I am a normal man for the first quarter of a mile; for the next hundred yards I am in a mild state of dread, controllable and controlled; for the next twenty yards in an acute state of dread, yet controlled; for the next ten, in an anguish of terror that hasn't reached the crisis of explosion; and in a half-dozen steps more I am in as fierce a panic of isolation from help and home and of immediate death as a man overboard in mid-Atlantic or on a window-ledge far up in a sky-scraper with flames lapping his shoulders.

'It is as scientific a fact as any I know that my phobic seizures at their worst approach any limits of terror that the human mind is capable of in the actual presence of death in its most horrible forms' (Leonard, 1928).

In the depths of despair in 1973, I knew that I would gladly have sold my soul to the devil for just one day of complete health. I would unhesitatingly have given away everything I had personally and professionally to anyone who could have guaranteed just 24 hours of normal health. It appeared at the time that there was no one who could help me, either in the human or supernatural categories.

To the agoraphobe who is a sincere Christian, it must appear the ultimate folly that after years or even decades of existing in a living hell, there still exists the possibility of going to an even worse hell after death. To the agoraphobe who has no religious convictions, it is all too apparent that the potential for heaven and hell already exists within you.

The terror of agoraphobia, which may seem all-enveloping at the time, actually can be subdivided into several distinct fear facets which are also heavily interlinked. To gain a proper understanding of what the agoraphobe is frightened of (and they frequently have little idea themselves), it is necessary to take a hard look at the various forms of their fears.

PANIC

Crippling phasic panic attacks are the most common hallmark of
agoraphobia and the most distressing experience it can offer. Logically, they are accompanied by all the signs of extreme anxiety:
palpitations, unsteadiness, quick, shallow breathing, weakness, and
feelings of impending death. Panic is recognised as the chief cause
for the failure of most agoraphobia treatments. Months of re-
habilitation can be undone by a few minutes of recurring panic
and repeated less severe attacks of anxiety can result in fears being
re-learnt.

When panic struck me, all common sense, reasoning and normality were blown to the winds in a blinding sheet of terror, which
deprived me of the ability or will to think, move or breathe
properly. I felt (and was) as white as a sheet, with every drop of
blood appearing to have drained out of my body; mouth dry, and
hands and body clammy with cold sweat. I do not recall that I
ever felt I was going to die or have a heart attack as do many
agoraphobes. On the whole, those two alternatives might well have
appealed too much at the time of panic, so perhaps my subconscious
protected my ultimate safety by never giving me those particular
fear facets.

Agoraphobia sufferers frequently have a continuous background
of anxiety regardless of environment; indeed the features of general
anxiety are closely linked with phobias. This can take the form
of 'free floating anxiety', which is an excellent description for
tensions and anxieties which can grip you more or less at any time.
No matter where you are or what you are doing, the free floating
anxiety is permanently there, pushing up the stress level, for no
apparently good reason. There is thus much fertile ground for the
development of panic attacks, but they can also happen without
any background of general anxiety at all—quite literally 'out of
the blue'.

The panic does not differ essentially from 'ordinary' panic when
a 'normal' person gets a bad fright. However, the panic can go on

longer, and it can appear without any of the stimulus necessary for a normal panic situation. It comes suddenly and can disappear as quickly as it came. Panic attacks can be few and far between, or they can strike as rapidly as shots from an automatic weapon. They can last for a few seconds, or a few minutes, and for some unfortunates they have been known to go on for nearly an hour.

Outside stimuli or circumstances appear to bear little relevance to panic, and an examination of internal stimuli within the person as a possible cause is almost equally as unsatisfactory. In a minority of cases the panic has been linked to individual personality problems, but it is doubtful if this offers much or any explanation for the majority of cases.

Most panic attacks can come at any time, day or night, although Isaac Marks suggests that the panics can be precipitated by stressful tasks (Marks, 1969). This latter observation links in well with the latest research into the causes of agoraphobia. (See pp. 160–162).

Even if hundreds of attacks have been experienced by the unfortunate person, it is important to appreciate that the panic feels just as bad as it did the first time. 'My God, I'm just as bad as I ever was! It is never going to let me alone. I may as well give up!' are typical feelings of an agoraphobe after any panic attack. It appears as though the person is forever doomed to go back to square one—no matter how hard he or she tries to fight their fears, the panic will get them in the end.

Agoraphobes react differently to panic attacks, some displaying the most literal interpretation of being 'scared stiff', their muscles being frozen by terror, or feeling so weak that they have to hang on to something or someone for support. I am not sure who panicked the most the first time I literally froze to the spot when Jim and I went to a local barbecue! I could not move, talk or even think, but just stood against a barn door, dumb with terror, with every cell in my body screaming to go home. Jim held conversations for both of us until I finally became mobile enough to stagger unnoticed to the car.

Accurately conveying the extremity of fear which agoraphobes endure is a daunting task. Even the agoraphobe finds it hard to accept, because he feels the 'ridiculousness' of his fear probably far more acutely than anyone else. To the onlooker and even to the doctor, the extent of the fear is most difficult to appreciate, when there is apparently nothing at all of which to be afraid. That 'nothing' can cause such panic is understandably almost incomprehensible to anyone who has not experienced it. However, Professor Leonard has only scorn for those who remark that 'nothing ever happens' when panic takes place. He points out that obviously the seizure happens, which is the equivalent of a red-hot iron being run down the throat, miraculously leaving no after-effects, and that the conscious mind is subjected to the acutest agony. The panic attacks left him even more prone to further attacks for weeks or months afterwards, and robbed him of a good part of what little freedom of outside movement he had managed to gain.

Although, statistically, agoraphobes rarely faint or collapse during panic attacks, Fleet Street journalist David recorded that sometimes through the intensity of fear he would faint. Stanley Law unwittingly describes a perfect example of the 'barber's chair syndrome' when he was completely overwhelmed by panic while having his hair cut, and he also records that he actually collapsed with fear in the street outside.

On the first half-day of a new job as an adult trainee journalist, I was so overcome with fear after being taken round the local calls by the assistant editor that I went blind. Apart from a tiny area on the periphery of my vision I was totally without sight, a symptom which I now know in retrospect was a negative scotoma, usually associated with migraine. In my ignorance at that time I got a very bad fright, and only the calm understanding of my therapist, whom I telephoned that lunchtime, persuaded me to return for the afternoon and sweat it through.

Agoraphobic panic is a torture of the most rarefied kind. It is something which is so terrible that I could never wish it on the most hated of men or women, even for the most horrible crimes against humanity. If a scientist could harness the massive energy being generated by panic attacks throughout the world at this moment, he might find that he held sufficient power to create a useful nuclear deterrent.

FEAR OF THE FEAR

Once the intensity of panic is appreciated to even a limited degree by non-agoraphobic people, it is easier to see how 'fear of the fear' develops as a logical sequence.

Consider an average non-neurotic person suddenly being confronted with a situation where panic blasts through them like a massive electric shock. Although the situation where it happens is going to be vividly remembered, the fear is not particularly of the situation itself, but of the terrible feelings which they experienced, and which they most certainly never wish to experience again. Avoidance of that particular situation is an obvious thing to do, but if it is unavoidable, the fear 'Is it going to happen again?' is never far from the person's mind. Even if they can avoid the place of their panic encounter, the same nagging question will be hovering over them wherever they are, since the first attack was probably completely illogical anyway. Panic can and does attack at any time and in any place.

Claire Weekes has recognised the importance of understanding the electrifying quality of panic for anyone attempting to treat agoraphobia. She claims it is the key to understanding how fear of it can arise in people who would not normally panic (Weekes, 1977).

In the first stages of my agoraphobic experience, my panics as such were few and far between. However, it was the fear of experiencing such an attack which made me loth to leave my home. I knew that once I had left my refuge, it was all 'just waiting for me' outside. With this fear constantly pounding away at me, my stress level would go sky high, even if I was at home. For at least three years I could not look at any traffic sequence on television, or listen to the traffic news on radio without coming out in a cold sweat of complete apprehension at what would happen to me if I was stuck in the traffic jam being described, or if I was driving down an open motorway (motorways are extremely difficult for agoraphobes since lines of retreat are comparatively few).

Fear of the fear is not just confined to agoraphobia, but associated with other phobias as well. To escape this added dread, the specific phobia sufferer will also avoid his particular phobic situation, often greatly curtailing his normal activities and life style. For instance, a person who is afraid of leaves will not willingly go out in autumn, or visit the countryside if he can help it. Similarly, the phobia sufferer will run through and through his particular fear in an agony of fearful anticipation over the next time he may run across the feared object or situation. Quite soon the phobia sufferer and the agoraphobe will start to see their fears in almost every shadow.

Rangell (1952) noted that the phobic patient almost becomes married to the phobic object: 'In order to avoid it his eyes seek it out, he finds it in obscure places, he sees it with his peripheral vision.' From this, it can be seen clearly how agoraphobic fears can gradually spread, encompassing a much greater field than that caused by the first scare. In severe agoraphobia, the fears have generally managed to permeate practically every conceivable situation.

I started with a fear of intercontinental travel, followed by fear of continental travel, then fear of travel in my own country, quickly followed by fear of travelling locally. The fear eventually encompassed going anywhere, covering all situations, effectively crippling all outside actions.

Vincent also points out that his malady came upon him gradually and went through definite stages of development, and that he was conscious of his affliction every minute that he was awake. (See p. 25.)

David describes how if he tried to cross a street and allowed the thought of fear to enter his head, terrible excitement and panic would seize him. He would reason with himself about his fears, but the moment he began to think 'Can I do this?' he was finished. He felt something break inside himself and, though he spurred himself like an unwilling horse being driven at a five-barred gate, he would back away again. Occasionally he did go through with it, but he described it as the most terrible agony. Professor Leonard also talks of the increase of his 'fear of the Fear' after a panic attack.

This helps to explain why an agoraphobe who is invited out on the spot for a short trip will be far more likely to be able to make the excursion than if someone telephoned and asked him to make the same trip in a week, a day, or even in an hour's time. There has been no chance for him to fully activate his fear of the fear, and going out naturally presents less problems.

Even seconds can build up the fear of the fear to epic proportions. For years, if my husband did not have the car ready to move the moment I was ready to make a dash for an outside destination, it took yet another round of courage building before I was ready to go. Another example from my own experience is being stopped in a car at traffic lights, or, worse still, at the painfully slow traffic lights one normally encounters at road works. I would quickly become overwhelmed with fear of panic striking while the car was stationary, and the sense of relief once the car started moving was quite indescribable.

Give an agoraphobe any chance to reflect on an invitation or an appointment in the near or far future, and they will probably die a thousand deaths in anticipation of all the horrors that might happen. It matters very little if the event outside is a pleasant or unpleasant one. The pressure of having to attend a beloved daughter's wedding, or a parent's funeral, and the fear of letting the family (and yourself) down can quickly assume monstrous proportions.

The actual event is often easier to tolerate than the anticipation of it. Towards the end of my agoraphobic experience, I found that my only real problem was the fear of the fear. I might quiver with fearful anticipation before an outside event, but the actual event, once underway, frequently presented no problems at all.

FEAR OF FEELING

Fear of the fear can also accurately be equated with 'fear of feeling'. As it is the dreadful feelings associated with panic which scare agoraphobes almost to death, and as all the symptoms are related to sensations of various kinds, fear of feeling is perhaps an even more accurate alternative or additional description of this particular facet.

It is worth reflecting on how little modern western society is encouraged to feel its natural feelings, and how often it is actively discouraged. Once early childhood is passed, crying, shouting, screaming with rage, wild shows of affection and other 'childish' acts are, for the most part, heavily frowned on. A child soon learns that it will not be popular if it continues showing its spontaneous emotions, and it begins to 'grow up' often by suppressing and fearing its real feelings.

The price we all pay is that the majority of our society finds it extremely difficult to tolerate its own emotions, or the emotions of others. Grief is often confined to a few hidden tears at a public funeral since others find it uncomfortable. Sedative drugs are regularly prescribed to bereaved people so that they cannot feel the full brunt of their grief. Men have as much right and ability to cry as women, and yet the reaction to a man in genuine grief will probably be one of acute embarrassment at his apparent 'unmanliness'.

We are all brought up to admire the strong, silent, 'stiff upper lip' character, and we would consider it most odd if the leaders of our society, the politicians, the businessmen, and the television personalities, suddenly started to say or do what they really felt, instead of what they know or are taught is acceptable to the majority. This general attitude, which fortunately is not confined to everyone in the western world, can result in a greater predisposition to psychological and psychosomatic (stress-induced) disorders.

Since toleration of feeling in many people may be low, due to simple social conditioning, they will be more prone to react severely to the first onslaught of agoraphobia. The actual experience of feelings on such a scale will be far beyond their capacity of toleration.

Being a typical product of western society, I found the humiliation of being forced to feel through agoraphobia a most difficult experience. When others were attending a lecture or a meeting with me, while they might appear to be relaxed and calm, I would be in a welter of emotions with wave after wave of panic engulfing me, hanging on by my fingernails hoping I could 'last' until the end of the meeting and not make a fool of myself, until perhaps I could stand the feelings no longer and would have to make an undignified (in my eyes) exit. As each wave flowed in, then ebbed away, I would become even more frightened of the next wave in case it might finally engulf me and I would 'explode' or lose control. The extra fear made sure that the next wave was even worse, making the final conclusion even more inevitable. If I survived one meeting, there was no guarantee that the next one would be any easier, the fear never abating and steadily growing.

Properly defined, agoraphobic panic is the fear of the fear of what might happen to you; the fear of the horrible feelings which will overwhelm you at the most inopportune time.

FEAR OF LOSS OF CONTROL

Fear of loss of control is probably one of the biggest factors in encouraging and precipitating a panic attack, and is a logical companion to the preceding fear of feeling. Although the National Survey of Agoraphobics gave less than eight per cent citing 'losing control' as their worst fear of what would happen during a panic attack, I believe the real figures are very much higher than this.

Aspects of loss of control include fear of fainting, collapsing, loss of memory, going insane, causing a scene, becoming hysterical and being physically ill, so virtually all the items mentioned in the survey could accurately come under this one umbrella description. (See p. 172.)

Again, the 'stiff upper lip' aspect of western society does not help the potential or actual agoraphobe, who acutely fears making a fool of himself. Feeling conspicuous is a real bugbear for him. 'What will people think?' he constantly asks himself. 'If I lose control, society will shun me forever as an acceptable human being.'

This fear of what other people will think can become quite paranoid, out of any proportion to the notice people are likely to take if a person faints, collapses, is sick, or has to go to the lavatory in a hurry. I know I felt as if there was a flashing neon sign on my forehead if my agoraphobic fears suddenly made it imperative that I went to the toilet.

The latent fear of going insane can give enormous impetus to the agoraphobe's fear of loss of control. The secret belief that you must be, have to be, a 'head case', with all the weird frights and illnesses you are experiencing, makes it paramount that tight control is maintained at all possible times. 'If I lose control, if I collapse or faint in the street, people will find out what I am like, and I will be taken to a mental home where I really know I belong,' runs the unfortunate person's mind, if he is not under the care of a psychiatric unit already.

In the public mind there remains a primitive fear of the stigma of mental illness, largely drawn from ignorance, bad publicity, and the bad conditions in many psychiatric units. To many people, psychiatric medicine is associated with 'head shrinking', drug taking, electric shocks and brain surgery. No wonder the average person, and agoraphobe, will try to steer clear of that if at all possible! I certainly did, and I fear that it will take many more years of enlightened education to root out the old attitudes to mental illnesses.

In the throes of fear, it does not occur to the terrified agoraphobe that the human race has been urinating, defaecating, fainting and being sick for millennia, without anyone noticing or thinking it peculiar, and in fact they are viewed as purely ordinary events.

It is very difficult for him to realise that the wracked agoraphobic body is not 'losing control', but is reacting very naturally to an extreme of panic—and it does not matter a hang what other people think. One of the greatest and most joyous of life's revelations to me was that no one, on the whole, could care a flea's whisker what you do—they are all far too busy getting on with their own lives.

A strict upbringing in childhood can help to sow the seeds for the potential agoraphobe by making him fear loss of control. Thankfully the keenness to make a child 'potty'-trained is now losing the fashionableness it had in the 1940s and 50s, and the modern child is being encouraged to get out of its nappies in its own time. A child that has had the importance of being 'dry' drummed into it from earliest childhood has been handed a real legacy of fear and shame by its parents, which will probably last until the day he or she dies.

A child who is told 'Mummy will not love you if you are sick again!' by its exasperated parent, will tend to react with shame and the conviction of public damnation if it gives in to its illness in the future. If parents ever realised the permanent damage they can cause by Victorian attitudes to the natural functions of the body, they would perhaps go down on their knees and rightly beg forgiveness from their anxiety-prone children.

Tackling the fear of losing control demands courage of the highest order from the agoraphobe. A person who is suffering from acute gastro-enteritis would never go out by choice. The prospect of being suddenly ill, or not being able to find a lavatory in time, would be more than enough to keep him safe in bed until he was better and in control of his stomach and bowels again.

No such luck for the agoraphobe, who may suffer, just as I did, from similarly acute symptoms of 'phantom' gastro-enteritis. You feel you are not in control of your body and that it will let you down at the worst possible moment, but you still have to face the awful prospect of going out if you are ever going to get better or have any sort of social existence.

For instance, as a newspaper reporter, I found the problems of attending crowded council meetings in stuffy committee rooms with no easy avenue of escape to be quite overwhelming, particularly when I had to leave the room for a fourth or fifth time to attend to the needs of acute panic! No one can ever know quite what agonies I went through, except perhaps my husband who saw the white, drained, speechless remnant of humanity who returned home after a night job of unremitting horror. On the other hand, one has to admit that true loss of control rarely happens. In all the years of my agoraphobia, I never once 'disgraced' myself in any way, but that in no way stopped the terrible fear of it happening the next time I went out.

Once the agoraphobe is able to lose control without panicking, he is well on the road to recovery. Loss of control is, after all, simply doing what you want to do as opposed to doing what you think you ought to do.

FEAR OF BEING TRAPPED

On the face of it, most of the agoraphobic symptoms such as feeling giddy and faint, getting 'jelly-legs' or feeling ill are events too common to bear much comment. To the agoraphobe, it is an entirely different matter, because any or all of those feelings can overwhelm him at just the 'wrong' moment—sitting on a bus, in the theatre or cinema, on a shopping trip, or in the middle of a business conference.

All the situations where panic strikes have one thing in common. The agoraphobe feels trapped and there is no respectable line of escape. That is why, as one agoraphobe put it, going shopping bears all the resemblance to planning a train robbery. Lines of escape must be worked out all the way, and as long as the 'rabbit runs' exist on any outing, it usually can be tolerated. Going on a strange journey, or even going to a strange house will present almost insurmountable difficulties since it is not always possible for the agoraphobe to work out escape routes in advance.

This is perhaps where the idea of 'fear of open spaces' became strongly associated with agoraphobia. Open spaces like wide fields and parks, wide streets and open tracts of land have no escape routes. You are totally exposed and there is nowhere to run.

As a farmer's wife, this aspect was particularly troublesome for me. The south-west Lancashire plain contains some of the most fertile land in the world, but it was small comfort at the time since the area is as flat as a pancake, with the sparse bent trees, continually battered by the prevailing westerly winds, providing very little cover. The modern farming policy of removing hedgerows to gain extra precious acreage was certainly no benefit to an agoraphobic farmer's wife. Winter was particularly hard to bear, since there were no leaves on the trees or hedges, and no high banks of weeds in ditches to retreat to if panic struck. I was noticeably worse with agoraphobia in winter than in summer, and the simple reason was the lack of foliage.

It can be deduced from this that there is no particular mystery why some agoraphobes can climb mountains but not walk in valleys, why some can go to the theatre, while others can manage shopping, why one route to work is possible and another is not. They can usually go where they feel reasonably certain that they can escape with ease if necessary, and everyone is different in their experiences.

In assessing an agoraphobe's fears, the behavioural aspect of panic situations must also be taken into account, where certain surroundings will always be more emotive than others, and where the fear of being trapped will noticeably be stronger.

One of the most difficult lessons an agoraphobe has to learn is that he never is trapped—there is always a way out of any situation. It is no good him knowing or accepting this fact without *feeling* the conviction to the roots of his being. Once his belief in this is sound, sincere and thoroughly worked out, he is well on the way out of the trap of agoraphobia.

PHYSICAL SYMPTOMS OF FEAR

In all the so-called 'mental' illnesses, agoraphobia must take pride of place for manifesting the most alarming physical symptoms. While I had agoraphobia, it gave me colitis (violent diarrhoea), vomiting, sweating, nausea, headaches, violent bodily pains, coughing, spots, rashes, blocked nasal passages, lumps, toothache, cramp, dizziness, blackouts, earache and even itchy ears!

The majority of agoraphobes are subject to varying degrees of physical symptoms. Common complaints are of nausea, dizziness, sea sickness, going weak at the knees, palpitations, hot and cold sweats, bodily pains, fainting (rarely), and sometimes actually being sick or dashing to the lavatory when the fear gets really bad. The fear of the horrible physical symptoms leaping on them, if they do have the courage to go out, is what keeps many agoraphobes at home.

I finally discovered that these alarming symptoms were totally stress induced (psychosomatic), although at the time of experiencing them, it was difficult to believe that the acute pain, illness, and discomfort had anything at all to do with a 'mental' problem. After a really bad day, I would occasionally seize up completely, paralleling my experience in Boston, unable to move any limb at all because of the extremely painful shooting pains which would inevitably result.

As I gradually became more self-aware, I noticed distinct correlations between my various physical and nervous symptoms. If I suppressed any aggression, I would get colitis, fear of cancer resulted in lumps, anger resulted in vomiting, repressed speech (fear of saying what I really felt) resulted in sore throats, sexual problems resulted in spots, rashes, blocked nasal passages and cramp, and suppression and frustration would result in coughing. As I began to understand the origin of some of the physical symptoms, I found that if I tackled the underlying problem (for example, let my anger out rather than keep it in), the physical symptoms would automatically disappear.

To the disbelievers (and I would certainly have been one prior to my agoraphobic experience), I can only say that I got to the stage where a violently itchy red rash could cover large areas of my legs within minutes, and could disappear as rapidly once I realised what was the psychological cause and remedied it! Psychosomatic illness (physical manifestation of mental stress) means rather more to me now than mere words in a book.

Stanley Law considered that the psychosomatic manifestations of his condition verged on the intolerable. He had pains in his head, stomach and chest, quirks of vision, nausea, palpitations, and acute auditory sensitivity.

Professor Leonard remarked that 25 years previous to writing he had considered himself a 'somatic freak' since no doctor ever seemed able to explain his pains. His physical symptoms included two years of unrelieved eye pain, body aches in thigh, arm and neck, pain in the left jaw for two weeks' duration, excruciating pain in the rectum, auditory sensitivity, extreme sensitivity to smells, and severe palpitations. Years later he came to the same realisation as the author that the pains were purely stress-induced and said: 'Indeed, if I get a new pain nowadays . . . I say to my wife, not, "I wonder what is the matter with me," but, "I wonder what that *means*" ' (Leonard, 1928).

Whether or not the reader agrees that the physical symptoms have a psychological basis is not too important. What is important to the agoraphobe is that people accept that the physical pain they are going through is 100 per cent as painful as the 'real' thing. The fact that there may not be any apparent physical basis for the acute intestinal pains or other symptoms is quite immaterial.

Finally, it should be stressed that agoraphobes should always insist on a full medical check for their physical symptoms. There is always the chance that there *is* an underlying organic cause as opposed to a psychological one, for their illness, and this chance should never be overlooked.

PHOBIAS WITHIN AGORAPHOBIA

As this chapter is devoted to explaining what the terror of agoraphobia actually feels like, some space should be given to describing 'the phobias within the phobia'. Taking into account that the specific phobia sufferer can feel just as acute terror as an agoraphobe when presented with the feared object or situation, one can begin to appreciate the complications of phobias additional to the existing fear of public places.

Within my agoraphobia, I suffered acutely from fear of enclosed spaces (claustrophobia), being alone (autophobia), cancer (cancerophobia), insects (entomophobia), strangers (xenophobia), germs (mikrophobia), dirt (mysophobia), spiders (arachnophobia), eating in public, hospitals, and being ill, to name but a few. A few of these pre-dated my agoraphobia, such as the fear of insects and fear of enclosed spaces, and the specific phobias were by no means constant in their occurrence or intensity while I had agoraphobia.

There seemed an element of unfairness to me that when I had made the supreme effort of going out, I could then be absolutely terrified by the appearance of a moth. As a child who suffered badly from a fear of spiders and moths, I knew that given the choice of entering a room containing a spider or a roaring lion, I would have opted for confronting the lion. Phobic fear knows no bounds.

Again, having got through the rigours of the agoraphobic day, to be subjected to irrational fears of cancer followed by such acute fear of hospitalisation that I nearly froze in panic at the mere thought, was to have fear stretched almost to snapping point.

Professor Leonard carefully dissects his varying phobias. In childhood he suffered badly from fears of darkness, thunderstorms, dogs, bodily pains and blood. Other phobias were of bells, stepping on a trestle bridge, a most acute fear of razors, fear of constipation, fear of being poisoned either by food or sleeping powders, fear of swallowing at all, fear of committing suicide (allied to his fear of razors), fear of having a heart attack through his racing pulse, fear of water and ice, 'shame-phobia', stage fright and acute fear of public speaking. Leonard emphasises that these other phobias were secondary to his central dominating phobia of distance, or agoraphobia:

'My mind found diabolically cunning ways of rationalizing all my terrors into secondary forms, pseudo-explanations, as plausible as horrific. For, not having the true explanation, the reason still insisted by its own instinctive urge upon some explanation. So it was with the innumerable phobias which beset me' (Leonard, 1928).

Stanley Law describes how, after his first two major panic attacks, his condition steadily deteriorated during that fateful summer. His whole being was full of fear, his phobias including fears of darkness, thunderstorms, dogs, swallowing or trying to swallow, poison, death and committing suicide.

The agoraphobes' fears can be seen to be almost universal and add tremendously to the complications of their condition. Small wonder that the fight through all the bewildering and overwhelming fears within the fear seems a virtually impossible task, both to the sufferers and to the doctor or therapist.

DEPERSONALISATION

When things really did go over the top and I could take no more agoraphobic punishment, nature provided me with a most necessary haven. I would quite simply and unconsciously cut off from my feelings, a process described by psychiatrists as 'depersonalisation'. Isaac Marks speculated that depersonalisation can sometimes be a switch or cut-off mechanism which is triggered when anxiety reaches a given level. As far as I am concerned, he need no longer speculate: it is a fact.

Depersonalisation refers to the changes in the person; derealisation refers to apparent changes in their surroundings. The psychiatric terms make the process sound more frightening than it really is. As many agoraphobes do suffer from depersonalisation at times (for example, 37 per cent in the 1962 study by Harper and Roth), it is important to stress that if this cut-off mechanism did not exist, the mind would really suffer a severe breakdown. One has only to imagine what would happen to a pressure cooker if the safety valve got blocked.

Depersonalisation is not a pleasant experience in anyone's book. I imagine it is somewhat similar to the sensations of those people who claim to have experienced clinical death and been able to see their own bodies from a few feet above, before returning to live in their 'corpses' once more.

The loneliness of depersonalisation is intense—after all, you have given up on everyone including yourself—and the pain and hurt is indescribable. Physically, I would not move, my blood flowed so slowly that my limbs were icy cold and my face quite white, and I could only see about a square inch in the centre of my normal range of vision. Everything around me became totally unreal, and I neither knew nor cared who or what anything was.

This can be an alarming time both for the agoraphobia sufferer and his family, but there is nothing to fear. Nature is providing a refuge, if a rather terrifying one, and inevitably the agoraphobe will always come back when the mind has run away for long enough.

CONCLUSION

Can agoraphobia kill, is a question which must have crossed the reader's mind while learning of the extremes of terror and despair which are encountered in this condition. The answer is quite simply that it can and does kill people.

In October 1979 inquests held on the same day gave suicide verdicts on two tragic agoraphobia cases. A Buxton mother took an overdose of tablets because she was so desperate about her 17-

year-long dread of going outdoors. A Liverpool agoraphobe killed herself at the fifth attempt by putting a plastic bag over her head because of her fear of stepping beyond the door of her home.

Putting up with the constant, dragging terror of agoraphobia saps energy on a massive scale. Whereas the average human being has sufficient energy to keep him going during the day, the agoraphobe has used up his quota almost before he starts. This results in every-day jobs assuming gigantic proportions, where even to put a load of washing in a machine seems an almost insuperable task. The vicious circle of stress and fear leading to tiredness, leading to more stress, and so on, means that an agoraphobe forcing himself to lead a 'normal' life is burning himself up at an enormous rate.

Vincent was astounded at the endurance of the human spirit in the face of the agony he had endured for so many years. This is a feeling certainly shared by myself. Journalism is scarcely suited to an agoraphobe, and after a day working in and out of an editorial office, the prospect of a night job in a crowded public place seemed unendurable, yet I always found sufficient reserves from some-where to do it. The cost was very high, but the prospect of not doing it was worse. When I got home, often at midnight, I was completely emotionally and physically finished, yet the next day had to be faced, and all the following ones, with no respite. When I was trapped in my home, it was not a haven to me. It was a prison, where agoraphobia marched around as relentlessly as ever.

It is completely misleading to think that once an agoraphobe has made his dash to safety, or even decides never to leave the sanctuary of his home, then everything feels fine. In my worst extremities of fear, I would sit in the office of my fairly isolated country home, with the curtains closed, stiff with the terror that someone might come. Every time the telephone rang, if there was a knock at the door, or if a car went past, I would run into the back of the house, and would not come out until Jim, if he was there, came to assure me that everything was safe.

Safe from what? From people invading my place of safety, which immediately became a 'public place' once visitors stepped over the threshold. Then there was nowhere else to go if I wanted to run, so the panic was doubly worse.

Nights can be almost worse than days for the agoraphobe, because, once you relax, that is when all hell lets loose. Once you remove the defences you have had up all day to keep you going, the gremlins can move in with ease, and I found the evening to be the worst time for getting cramp, toothache, and all the other aches and pains my subconscious had lined up for me.

Even in sleep, agoraphobia holds hands tenaciously with the Sandman. I would wake up in the morning, utterly worn out with agoraphobic dreams of being on coaches, in traffic jams, losing control, and never being able to find a lavatory, which went on unremittingly for four years.

Vincent concludes: 'I see a man hobbling past my house on crutches, a cripple for life, and I actually envy him. At times I would gladly exchange places with the humblest day-labourer who walks unafraid across the public square or saunters tranquilly over the viaduct on his way home after the day's work' ((Anon) Vincent, 1919).

In my time I have almost prayed to be made physically disabled, a state which seemed desirable compared to the baffling terror of the equally disabled agoraphobe, who gets far less sympathy from an equally baffled world.

No one deserves agoraphobia, although it might be a temptation to let everyone in the world experience it for just one day. After that, their total appreciation of being able to lead a normal life would lead most certainly to a much happier and more peaceful global existence.

REFERENCES

(Anon) Vincent (1919). Confessions of an Agoraphobic Victim. *American Journal of Psychology*, 30, 299.
Harper, M. and Roth, M. (1962). Temporal Lobe Epilepsy and the Phobia-anxiety-depersonalisation Syndrome. *Comprehensive Psychiatry*, 3, 129–151.

Leonard, William E. (1928). *The Locomotive God*, p. 322. Chapman and Hall, London.

ibid, p. 251.

ibid, p. 320.

Marks, Isaac M. (1969). *Fears and Phobias*, p. 137. William Heinemann Medical Books, London.

Rangell, L. (1952). The Analysis of a Doll Phobia. *International Journal of Psychoanalysis*, 33, 43.

Weekes, Claire (1977). *Agoraphobia. Simple, Effective Treatment*, p. 21. Angus and Robertson, London.

Chapter 4

Agoraphobia and the Family

'Your agoraphobia is the best thing which has ever happened to us,' Jim remarked one day when I was half-way along the road to recovery. Certainly, agoraphobia creates a make-or-break situation with husbands, wives, family and friends, and I was lucky. Without Jim's constant and sympathetic support, my recovery would have taken much longer to achieve. The years of trauma drew us closer together and the violence of agoraphobia which ripped me down to my foundations gave us both a very special insight into the workings of the human mind. Not everyone is so fortunate, and the social side of living with agoraphobia deserves much strong comment.

If you multiply the minimum half million agoraphobes in the United Kingdom by the size of an average family, there are already two million people in this country who are directly affected by the results of having an agoraphobia sufferer in their midst. Add one or two friends, neighbours, or business colleagues, and the numbers begin to look astronomical. With literally millions of people affected one way or another by agoraphobia the social problems of agoraphobia begin to assume massive proportions. In view of the numbers involved, one may wonder why so little has been done for agoraphobia compared to other modern scourges, like cancer or heart disease.

The answer is fairly simple. By his very nature the agoraphobe cannot parade down Whitehall shouting for the help which he needs. He may not even be able to get out of his home to vote for his Member of Parliament, let alone lobby him for more action from the Department of Health. The agoraphobe's acute desire for anonymity also works against any extra notice being given to the problem, and with mental health taking a back seat to all other aspects of medicine, the prospect of Government action is dim indeed.

Brave attempts have been and continue to be made by agoraphobes to utilise the normal avenues of pressure. Only recently I listened to a promise of an interview with an agoraphobe on the radio, and that was the last that was heard of it. A feature on phobias on television ended with an apology for an agoraphobe who had failed to make it to the studio. What agonies those poor folk must have gone through!

Being interviewed by the media, and especially getting to a radio or television studio, presents devastating problems to the agoraphobe. An average person would find the prospect of an interview, even with a local newspaper, fairly daunting. Add a dash of agoraphobic fears and the interview becomes nearly an impossibility.

In 1971 four terrified women made the most nerve-wracking pilgrimage of their lives to hand in a petition at 10 Downing Street. It was presented by a 53-year-old London mother who was fortified by tranquillisers to help her survive the most testing ordeal of her life. They asked the Prime Minister to help promote more help and understanding for agoraphobia sufferers. As recently as June 1979, 60 agoraphobes defied their illness and converged on the House of Commons seeking support from the Government and Opposition for their cause.

In the last decade or so the excellent work of the various phobic organisations, particularly The Open Door Association founded in 1965 and the newer Phobics Society, has gained some much needed help and recognition for the problem. At least agoraphobes now have the opportunity of knowing the rights and benefits to which they are entitled. For instance, a housebound person can apply for such things as a heating allowance, he can qualify to vote by proxy at local and Parliamentary elections, and he can apply to his Family Practitioner Committee for a dentist to treat him at home. New and helpful information relating to phobic illness and its treatment is constantly being disseminated through the chatty and heartwarming newsletters of phobic organisations. (See 'Useful Addresses' p. 193.)

One MP who launched a campaign in Parliament to help agoraphobia sufferers was Mr Greville Janner, Labour MP for Leicester North-West who accurately summed up the situation. He said: 'These unfortunates and their families have nightmarish lives. The numbers are vast but little is done. The Government does not spend enough money, there is not enough research, and the few self-help organisations are hampered by lack of funds. We are just sweeping the problem under the carpet' (*News of the World*, 9 April 1972).

IMPACT ON THE FAMILY

The impact of agoraphobia on the family is all-encompassing. As most agoraphobes live with their families, inevitably everyone is affected to a greater or lesser degree. Certainly the family's life will never be the same again once agoraphobia is in residence in the home.

The effect on a family with an agoraphobic or semi-agoraphobic member can be as difficult as that of looking after someone who is badly physically disabled. Perhaps it is worse, because it is very hard for a non-agoraphobic person to accept that someone who is apparently sound in wind and limb cannot do anything or go anywhere outside his immediate surroundings. The millions of people who have to contend with having an agoraphobia sufferer in their midst deserve the strongest support and help from outside agencies such as local government and medical and social organisations. The chances are that they will receive little or no help from anyone and they will be left to cope as best they can.

The families and friends of agoraphobes have a difficult and sometimes overwhelming task confronting them. Besides putting up with the day-to-day practical problems of agoraphobia, such as making sure the agoraphobe is not left on his own, doing all the outside chores, taking the children to school, they are asked to show unlimited patience, have a ready ear for apparently endless agoraphobic grumbles of 'how dreadful it is', give perennial encouragement no matter how many failures occur, and give constant reassurance that they still love the afflicted person.

As agoraphobes generally feel easier when accompanied by a trusted companion, and as many agoraphobes are afraid of being left alone, this places a great deal of strain on relatives and friends. An agoraphobe is scarcely the most cheerful person to have around, and it can have a very depressing effect on family life, when the demands and dependency of agoraphobia have to be catered for constantly.

While I was agoraphobic, Jim had to do all the shopping on top of his normal farming workload. He came home to a terrified person, so worn out with the tensions of the day that he often had to get the evening meal ready. He could not have a holiday away from home, and if he went away on business, he had a wife almost beside herself with fright. He could not invite anyone casually into the house and somehow had to get rid of visitors and friends when I could no longer tolerate their presence in my home. He had to put up with the worst of my bad temper, depression, hopelessness and bitterness because he was the only person on whom I could vent it.

Fortunately we did not have children, for I could scarcely cope with myself, let alone a family. Agoraphobic parents who manage to cope with some semblance of family life are heroes and heroines indeed—and so are their families, if they extend, as so many do, the love and patience which are so necessary for getting better.

Like most agoraphobes, my condition meant that our social life became virtually non-existent. Before either of us had any conception of what agoraphobia entailed, we went on a last and disastrous holiday to the Lake District. Jim was irritated throughout the vacation by my extreme reluctance to travel anywhere, and I was irritated because I was doing my darnedest to get over my peculiar fears. The fears became worse, and our next attempt at getting away for a weekend came to a sudden halt on top of Parbold Hill, a few miles away from home. My panic drove us home and we sat with our suitcases in the house for some time, saying nothing. We were both too despondent for words.

The same summer, Jim decided that we could attempt a holiday on a longboat on the local Leeds/Liverpool canal which runs through our land. We went with a number of friends, and with toilet facilities on board, Jim felt that I would have no problems; I certainly had my fingers crossed. This ended in disaster as well, because I did not realise that the congestion of people on board and the silence of the night would combine to accelerate my fears. Overwhelmed with panic in the small hours, I rushed home the next day much to Jim's disgust. The whole exercise had become a complete nightmare, for under such favourable conditions and among friends I had failed, and it proved to me that I could no longer function as a normal human being.

Prior to agoraphobia I had done a lot of business and social entertaining both at work and at home, with people often staying overnight. Friends and acquaintances suddenly found that they were no longer welcome. A Pembroke farmer and his wife were put off at the last minute from coming to see us because I completely funked the prospect of having them at home. As they had once given us a lovely holiday, Jim was naturally furious and he was further aggravated because I forced him to make excuses for my baffling and hurtful behaviour.

On a very few occasions I simply could not get out of putting up friends for the night. That epitomised the final onslaught on my place of retreat. I sweated and shook with terror throughout the night of their stay, terrified of losing control in the quietness. Finally the bizarre situation occurred where I would request visitors to pitch their tents in the garden, or sleep in the billiards room which was separate from the main house. To this day, I have no idea what they thought, but it is amazing how unquestioning people are in the face of odd behaviour.

The ability to cope with other people in the house extended to the farm dog. Flint, our most friendly Rhodesian ridgeback, used his other farmyard homes for sleeping during the worst of my agoraphobia. I had to be alone to cope with the raging terrors within myself which could become almost demonic at night.

Things could get a lot worse when I became acutely hypersensitive, unable to stand noise, movement, touch, watching television, the feel of the sheets on my bed, or even the feel of the hair on my head. It was rather like living with an electrified hedgehog for Jim, and I would sweat out the worst nights on my own, unable and unfit to be with either man or beast. I do not doubt that things are just as bad if not worse for other agoraphobes and their families.

Many studies have been done on the effect of agoraphobia on the family, particularly on marriage. A general statistical commentary is given in the Appendix on p. 177, but a point which does emerge most strongly is that the attitude of the marriage partner can have a significant effect on the successful treatment of the agoraphobe.

Unstable or unsatisfactory marriages tend to get worse as the agoraphobe gets better. Conversely, strong partnerships can improve as recovery commences. Doctors and therapists have noted that agoraphobes from unsatisfactory marriages are much more reliant on them for any improvement, and as soon as their therapeutic help is withdrawn, relapse can quickly follow. Agoraphobes with good marriages are far less dependent on their doctors as they work towards getting back to a normal life.

Marriages can and do break up once an agoraphobe has regained his freedom, because the flowering of the personality which takes place may prove too much for either partner. The abnormally jealous person may begin to accuse the agoraphobe of imagined infidelities as his ability to travel is increased. The partner can also begin very subtly to undermine the agoraphobe's confidence in order to keep him at home. Another form of blackmail that has been used is for the marriage partner to start having psychosomatic illnesses in order to make sure the agoraphobe stays put. Their partner's agoraphobia may have provided a very convenient excuse or camouflage for their own mild social phobias, and in this case they will not welcome it when recovery forces them to resume a normal social life, and will work against it.

From these observations, the agoraphobe may feel slightly wary about the results of getting better—it may not be such a bed of roses if he stands a chance of losing his partner in the process. Similarly the non-agoraphobic partner may feel slightly apprehensive, but this should not deter them.

Marriages which deserve to fail may well fail, but where both partners have worked through the agoraphobia together, sharing the ups and downs, their relationship will blossom and mature, bringing a great deal of extra understanding and happiness to both. What is to be gained far outweighs anything which may be lost on the way out of agoraphobia.

SOCIAL EFFECTS ON THE AGORAPHOBE

'My life has never been the same again' is a phrase used regularly by agoraphobes when describing the social effects of agoraphobia. The National Survey of Agoraphobics verified this observation when it asked its subjects to list the most detrimental effects their condition had had on their lives. The most popular choice was lack of social contacts, followed by personal or psychological effects such as feeling inferior or lacking in self-confidence, inability to work, problems in marital relations and travel restrictions. Oddly, little over five per cent listed guilt feelings about how agoraphobia might affect their children's development, although in most written interviews with agoraphobes this is usually mentioned (Burns and Thorpe, 1977a).

Agoraphobia presented me with the most peculiar social problems. I could not go to the cinema, theatre, restaurants or even the local pub. Dances and socials of any description were out of the question. Not only was I unable to visit my friends' homes, I could not even go to see my parents, who lived only a quarter of an hour's drive away. I could not go shopping, which meant I could not go out to buy my own underclothes, or even pop out for a loaf of bread. Family events like weddings, christenings and funerals were impossible, and even when my mother was in hospital for major surgery, there was no way I could have got to see her. Even if your loved ones are dying, agoraphobia has the absolute power to keep you at home.

Indeed one of the major handicaps for me, as it is for many other agoraphobes, was that I could not go to see a doctor or go to hospital under any circumstances, except perhaps unconsciousness! Few people feel very comfortable in a doctor's waiting-room, and for an agoraphobe it is virtually impossible to sit quietly in a room full of other anxious people. Similarly, going to the dentist was a potential nightmare. My dentist happened also to be a family friend, but it was a very long time before I summoned up the courage to tell him what was the matter with me. Only when I had reached complete desperation did I telephone him and say that I was frightened to come for my appointment because I had agoraphobia. He accepted it, telling me to come when I could, and I got there that time by crying my eyes out all the way. I found that once feelings start to be released in any form, the agoraphobic symptoms begin to subside.

Farmer's wives are used for emergencies by their husbands: doing the running around for paperwork, picking up spare parts, answering telephones and delivering messages, while their better halves get on with the work on the land. As a farmer's wife, I found my agoraphobia prevented me from taking the men a drink in the fields, and I was constantly terrified of being asked to drive Jim to the home farm, a matter of half a mile away. I could do only what little there was inside the house, and the sense of futility when I could not go out even for my own vegetables was very disheartening.

I was not alone in my social plight—so many other agoraphobes can tell equally if not more disturbing stories.

The social situation of a South London housewife who had agoraphobia for 23 years could certainly be described as desperate. Her normal life jerked to a sudden stop the day she felt faint, dropped her purse and fled in blind panic from the corner shop. For an incredible 10 years afterwards she was too frightened even to leave her bedroom. Eventually she attempted to leave the house at night under cover of darkness, but failed. When she made the supreme effort to go and see her married daughter, her legs refused to carry her into her daughter's house, and all the family could do was give her a cup of tea in the car during her visit.

The practical problems her agoraphobia caused were tremendous. She had to pay for someone to take her children to school, and she could never take them on holiday herself. Her grief was very deep when she was unable to attend the weddings of the eldest. When she needed a dentist, he had to come to her home, which proved very expensive, so when three other teeth needed extracting, she did it herself.

A woman from Rodley, near Leeds, had agoraphobia for 33 years. Throughout her married life she had never known what it was like to take her two children to the park, to go shopping for their clothes, or to attend school concerts, open days and speech nights. When her children were younger, they did not understand what was the matter with her and were easily hurt, especially when other children told them that their mother was lazy. Agoraphobia meant that she had very few friends since people soon tired of one-way visits all the time, and thought she ought to snap out of her illness.

Both these women were active, extrovert, fun-loving people before agoraphobia sliced through their existences like a giant meat-cleaver.

A London agoraphobe in her early 20s said: 'I cannot go shopping alone and often when I go accompanied I rush around as fast as is physically possible. I never go to anybody's house to eat because of the constant fear of being sick. I feel despair in myself when I go out of the house full of confidence, only to return like an unset jelly. All agoraphobes know how ridiculous all these things are, but I'm afraid to us they are very real.'

SOCIAL ATTITUDES TO AGORAPHOBIA

The reaction of family and friends to the agoraphobe is very variable, and depends very much on themselves and their circumstances. Undoubtedly, money and an educated background help to ease friction since both can be used to help cope with the disabilities and provide better medical treatment for the agoraphobe. I was very fortunate that I had both. A poorer and disadvantaged background, where family problems may already exist, can result in agoraphobia being used as a further battle-weapon. The person may intensify his symptoms more than is necessary, receiving no support at all from his family and very little medical help.

A Welsh agoraphobe told me: 'Relatives! Yes I have them, but since I've been agoraphobic I don't know them, or they don't want to know me. Neighbours still don't understand and they all think it's a mental disease, so give me a wide berth. The only time I see or speak to a neighbour is if they want to use my telephone. If it wasn't for my telephone I think we'd really starve.'

An agoraphobe from North Lancing gave a very different view: 'Although it obviously irritated my daughter she never stopped asking me to accompany her on shopping jaunts, and we began to accept the trouble and sort of make a joke about it. I would say "Here we go again!" as I hurried from a shop. We would travel to anywhere with all the windows open in the car or I would feel I couldn't breathe. Coming home we were able to keep them closed and not freeze.'

What agoraphobia does do is that it shows you very clearly who are your real friends—the ones who genuinely accept you for yourself. The results can be totally unexpected, with the most unlikely people standing by you through thick and thin, and others you previously would have staked your life on helping you, leaving you completely in the cold. The people who liked you originally for your professional status, social standing or material possessions will soon be lost in the rising tide of agoraphobia, and there is no need to mourn their disappearance.

I never expected any friend or acquaintance who knew I was agoraphobic to understand—after all, I did not understand it either. However, I did expect them to accept my condition and, not surprisingly, I was sometimes disappointed. I discovered that some acquaintances definitely preferred me in a dependent and failed situation, and as I began to recover, so their friendship was withdrawn. Few people wished to discuss what was wrong with me, because agoraphobia is rather like cancer or other forms of mental illness, it is an uncomfortable conversation piece. As I battled my way out of agoraphobia, I found some acquaintances actively tried to make things worse for me, or would sneer at the treatment which was obviously beginning to be beneficial.

Once outsiders start to attack in this way, the agoraphobe can be sure he is well on the road to getting better. As most people can be slightly agoraphobic, this reaction probably comes because they see the agoraphobe overcoming his difficulties, which leaves them with little excuse for putting up with their own minor agoraphobic problems. The reaction would appear to stem from fear, ignorance and a peculiar form of envy.

The majority of people can exist with their minor neuroses, but the agoraphobe cannot do so. Once he is better, his freedom, of necessity, is going to be more complete than for most.

It is worth remembering that agoraphobia, like all other phobias, is self-inflicted. Psychologically speaking, the inner self is so frightened that it has to find some 'thing' to make sense of its fright, and it is fairly arbitrary what this is going to be. I adore travelling, meeting people and seeing new places, but I suddenly found that my body and mind would not let me do those things any more.

Because agoraphobia is self-inflicted, albeit unconsciously, it becomes all the more easy for exasperated friends to tell you 'there's nothing to be afraid of', to 'get a hold of yourself' and all the other meaningless cant. As agoraphobia is a self-made trap, it is all the stronger and all the more difficult to break down since you are ultimately fighting and coming to terms with yourself.

Family, friends and doctors can do a great deal of harm by constantly exhorting the sufferer to 'pull yourself together', blaming the agoraphobe for his condition, and driving up the stress level still further by intensifying the person's all-too-ready guilt feelings about the illness. Indeed, if there is anything which drives an agoraphobe wild with fury or fills him with inner helplessness, it is the ludicrous insistence by both ill- and well-meaning people that he should pull himself together. If it was humanly possible for an agoraphobe to pull himself together, he would have done it long ago. There is no way he can possibly do it, so family, friends and doctors should cease to demand what he cannot supply. All such statements do is add to the aggravation of the problem, reinforce the person's feelings of inadequacy, actually reduce their courage in the face of their fears, and worsen the agoraphobia.

Shouting at the sufferer, forcing him to go out, scoffing at his fears, and leaving him in exasperation, have just the same result. The agoraphobia will become worse because the family has heightened the stress level.

There is no easy way out for the agoraphobe's family and friends, but I would offer them this advice.

Always retain your common sense in the face of agoraphobia. The agoraphobe does not need pity, but understanding and acceptance, which are vastly different things. Encouraging an agoraphobe to give into his fears can be equally as harmful as trying to force him out. Accept the agoraphobe's failures in exactly the same spirit that you would accept his successes; it will be shown later that it is necessary for the agoraphobe to get worse in order to get better.

Agoraphobia is bound to affect family life, perhaps severely, but never allow it to take over completely. Non-agoraphobic members of the family should take a break when they can, and they should take a holiday if possible—two nervous wrecks are not better than one. If the family manages to arrange things so that life goes on as normally as possible, the agoraphobe usually welcomes this because it eases his own burden of guilt.

Remember that a vital ingredient of getting well from agoraphobia is the will to get better. Encourage this in the agoraphobe and you will never have any cause for regret. Agoraphobes are not weak, but extremely tough, so give every help when it is necessary and do not hold back the healing process by becoming an unnecessary crutch. It can be unkind and cruel to make someone dependent who would otherwise be more independent. Talking

about fear often helps to lower the stress level and so ease agoraphobia, so it is to everyone's advantage if a ready ear is available
for the sufferer's woes, even though it can get very wearing.

Clinical depression, as opposed to normal depression, is frequently associated with agoraphobia, although you can have agoraphobia without being depressed. When depression is there, it is
characterised by hopelessness, crying, irritability, loss of interest
in work and family, insomnia, high anxiety and sometimes suicidal
thoughts. Depression adds a drab, grey, meaningless chill to every
day for the agoraphobe, and it can bring an aura of hopelessness to
the family who have to watch this unhappiness, which is of a
depth they cannot begin to understand or appreciate. Neither does
the agoraphobe or any other depressive understand why he feels
so miserable and why he dreads waking up each morning to face
yet another dreadful day. The agoraphobe and his family must keep
in mind that depression is an illness and that it can be cured.
Blaming the agoraphobe for the dragging listlessness of depression
will only aggravate the condition. Acceptance of the depression is
again the best and easiest policy, giving positive help when necessary, and allowing the person to feel depressed when the black
clouds move in.

The exhaustion of depression which can start almost before the
day begins is a very genuine thing and is in no sense malingering.
Common sense should again be used in encouraging the sufferer
to get sufficient rest, yet not lie in bed all day hoping that the world
will come to an end. When there are breaks in the clouds, make
sure the light shines in for as long as possible before the next bout
of depression. Take a positive attitude to whatever treatment is
being prescribed for depression and encourage the sufferer to stick
to it, because his energy and motivation level will be at an all-time
low.

Above all, agoraphobia is curable and it should no longer be regarded by the agoraphobe's family as a life sentence. A big danger
lies in accepting agoraphobia as a permanent feature of family life
and making no attempt to remove it. If that is allowed to happen

then that family and agoraphobe are well and truly sunk as far as getting better is concerned.

Jim observed: 'I found the most important thing for helping you through agoraphobia was discussing everything as we went along. I know agoraphobia looks very self-centred, with the person being continually obsessed with what is happening to them, but it made me look at everything in a different light. It made me question everything and not accept anything as I did before, and it expanded my own view of life.

'Acceptance of your agoraphobia was another very important thing I had to do. As most agoraphobes are married women, it must be very difficult if their husbands attack their agoraphobia instead of accepting it. For instance, if your agoraphobia meant I had to abandon a trip out at the last minute, I just accepted it. I accepted it just the same if we did manage to go out and enjoy ourselves. I stopped making any plans and just lived from day to day, which has turned out to be a far more satisfactory way of living than following the social pressures which I had never questioned before.'

It demands the highest courage and determination to combat agoraphobia, and the family and friends who give wholehearted support to the sufferer have everything to gain and certainly nothing to lose. Indeed, they may well find their own lives are greatly enriched in the process.

THE GOOD AND BAD DAYS

What makes agoraphobia so difficult to accept and understand is its fluctuating nature: some days are definitely easier than others in the ebb and flow of fear. When talking to agoraphobia sufferers or reading accounts of their illness, it is always apparent that their condition varies. They are never totally incapacitated all the time. It is this slight occasional detensification of their symptoms which gives them the opportunity to do some household job which had seemed too much to attempt the day before, to make an effort to go out or to increase the distance they can travel from home. In the worst extremes of my agoraphobia there were always days when I was not completely housebound, when I was less frightened of people, and when I did manage to complete the household chores.

The fluctuating nature of agoraphobia, which can be intensified and detensified by the smallest thing and sometimes nothing at all, is a real killer of social life. If I managed to get to a friend's house once, it made refusing an invitation to go again—because I felt I could not make it—doubly difficult. You are naturally considered to be lily-livered if you can face one evening out fairly well but not the next. The friend is bound to feel insulted, and invitations soon dry up.

The ups and downs of agoraphobia inevitably result in family and friends suspecting that agoraphobia is not an illness at all, and is more likely the result of laziness, lack of resolution, or a convenient excuse for avoiding awkward situations. In this situation the agoraphobe cannot win. If he survives a panic situation once, by summoning up every scrap of energy and resource at his command, his family will expect him to be able to cope again, and may even resort to forcing him out.

Most people can perform unexpected feats of courage in an acute crisis, but no one would expect them to do so several times a day. It is very important for the agoraphobe that his family appreciates this, and realises that going out really does demand such genuine heights of courage again and again. It is unrealistic and downright cruel to expect their agoraphobic member to do it all the time. In fact, the family will find that their unreasonable attitude will backfire on them and achieve the opposite of what they want. The added pressure they are putting on the agoraphobe will result in his stress level going sky-high a lot faster, and the agoraphobia will become a lot worse.

The problems of fluctuating agoraphobia actually increase as the agoraphobe begins to get better. Covering council meetings on my newspaper 'patch' in West Lancashire, I would find that I could get through a parish meeting with relative ease one month, and be absolutely dreadful the next. I would quite enjoy company one evening, and be very sick on the next occasion. I would face my fears with comparative equanimity one day, and be back to a panic-ridden agoraphobe for the following week. It was hopeless trying to explain the situation to anyone, and I finally learned that there is no necessity to try and explain agoraphobia. You know it exists, and that is all that matters.

The reason agoraphobic symptoms tend to fluctuate is that the human body and mind is incapable of panicking all the time. Periods of comparative calm come to even the most battered agoraphobe, although it may not feel like calmness to him. The most one can claim for the severe agoraphobe is that occasionally their suffering is slightly less harrowing than at other times. If an agoraphobe is sufficiently distracted or stimulated, it is also possible for him to forget his symptoms for a short while.

SOCIAL PLOYS AND PREFERENCES

As long ago as 1871, C. Westphal, the man who first coined the word 'agoraphobia', had noted how sufferers used tricks and ploys to help them through their social problems. Describing three male patients who feared going into streets and public places, he said: 'The subjects experienced great comfort from the companionship of men or even an inanimate object, such as a vehicle or a cane. The use of beer or wine also allowed the patient to pass through the feared locality with comparative comfort. One man even sought, without immoral motives, the companionship of a prostitute as far as his own door.'

The studies of Isaac Marks and others have shown that Westphal's observations apply equally to modern cases of agoraphobia. Agoraphobes in general feel easier when accompanied by a trusted companion, and this need not be a human friend, but can be an animal or even an inanimate object.

Stratagems which are commonly used include gripping a walking stick or umbrella, holding a suitcase, putting a folded newspaper under your arm, or pushing anything on wheels such as a bicycle or shopping trolley. A pet animal can prove quite indispensable if it can be taken out on a lead.

Vincent found carrying a suitcase or travelling bag helped him walk down a street, and that he could ride a bicycle with comparative ease in places where it would have been agony for him to walk.

Professor Leonard used several ploys to try and stave off his first major attack of agoraphobia. He drank beer, he tried to chat about irrelevancies, and finally he smashed a wooden box to pieces, board by board, against his knee to try and occupy himself against his panic. He failed completely. When his phobia made moving house closer to the university a necessity, the Professor used everything he had got to get over the 'grotesque bustle' of moving. His cottage had become such an acute centre of security for him, that to strip it of its familiar interior was to leave him completely lost. He only managed to get over this problem by carefully selecting articles which were put up in his next home by friends prior to his arrival. He spent the last night at the cottage surrounded by enough household articles to make it still look like home. Before the removal men came on the second day, his friends rushed him down to his new centre of security where other friends were ready to welcome him and his wife.

The newsman David vividly described his 'razor-edge' existence, where his ploys could take most dramatic forms. He once leapt on to a passing lorry to go over an open space near his editorial office, to the great amusement of his colleagues who were watching from the windows. Another time he was seized with panic in an open space, so dashed to help a hawker push a heavily laden wagon up the steep road, thus securing safety and a shelter for himself.

The agoraphobe's need to hold on to something stems from two major facts. One is that the object helps you to stay in touch with reality. The newspapers, shopping baskets, and so on, keep reminding you that you are part of the normal world, and the awful feelings of unreality are kept at bay. The second reason is that if you do start to feel giddy or unreal, you have something to grasp and even support you, particularly in the case of perambulators and bicycles. The object affords some sort of security which you can take out with you beyond the safe confines of home, and which will be with you whatever else happens. You might also feel that a certain object brings you 'luck', and with it panic is less likely to strike.

I developed my own 'tricks' to keep me going in social situations. I must have sucked a fortune in Polo mints, which gave my dry mouth something to do in panicky moments. I would also clench and unclench my toes to battle unseen against the ebb and flow of terror attacks. I made free use of alcohol to help damp down my anxiety. Despite its many critics, alcohol was a boon, since time and again it saved me from reaching the stress pitch where my agoraphobic symptoms would take over.

I have no illusions about the terrible damage alcohol can do when a person is an alcoholic. However, for the rest of humanity who are not alcoholics, drink can provide a most necessary safety valve from the stresses of everyday living. The anti-smoking and -drinking lobbies would do well to reflect on the fact that although cigarettes and alcohol can and do cause damage to health, stress is an even more lethal killer. If alcohol and tobacco are removed from the public's grasp, it will inevitably turn to something else to help relieve its anxieties. A great warning sign is the colossal number of drugs which are being consumed legally everyday to help keep western society on an even keel: for example, in 1979 a staggering 25 million prescriptions for tranquillisers were dispensed in Britain.

A big point in favour of alcohol is that unlike drugs it is socially acceptable. The local public houses played an important part in my recovery, since they were the first places I managed to reach; and the reason I managed to make it to the Red Lion and the Kicking Donkey (both less than a mile from home) was that I knew I could artificially control my stress symptoms once I got there—a polite way of saying I immediately had a large whisky! Meetings with other people first became possible in a pub for the same reason.

As long as an agoraphobe knows why he is using alcohol, there is not much danger of becoming alcoholic. Once the anxiety has dissipated, the need for alcohol evaporates as well. It is true that a small number of agoraphobes have become addicted to drugs and alcohol, but it is very much a minority. However, one study of 102 alcoholics attending a treatment unit in the north-east of England found that a third (33) suffered from agoraphobia and/or social phobia (Mullaney and Trippett, 1979).

Like many agoraphobes, I found I got fairly proficient at telling 'white' lies—untruths which would hurt no one, but helped me— saying I was bored, or had a headache, or had an urgent appointment somewhere else, in order to get away 'gracefully' from a panicky situation.

If David panicked when approaching an open square, he would suddenly remember a forgotten letter and have to go home for it, or, if the worst happened, he would pretend to be ill and call a cab. Leonard described how he concealed his phobia with the invention of all sorts of ingenious excuses for not attending conventions or any other invitations out of town. When agoraphobia hit Stanley Law during a cricket game, sometimes leaving him paralysed and breathless, he would retire temporarily from the game pleading a pulled muscle.

All the time the agoraphobe is looking round for somewhere he can rest his eyes, or for something which will take his mind off his horrible feelings. I would gaze at the rings on my fingers—watching how the gem-facets sparkled and twinkled in the light—when the surroundings were becoming too much. Similarly, I might gaze at a painting or an interesting bit of damp on a wall, or watch the sheen on a glass; anything to keep the other feelings from over- whelming me. The common factor in all the things I chose to look at is that none of them moved, so causing less stress to the eye, and keeping the tension level stable.

The main object of all the little tricks and ploys used by agora- phobes is fairly obvious. They seek to lower the tension level of their agoraphobia by any means possible, and any straw will be grasped with fervour. This is undoubtedly why social ploys can take such bizarre forms. Isaac Marks cites various case histories where a man had to remove his belt whenever he had an anxiety attack; a woman had to strip off all her clothes when she panicked and could only wear garments with zips in the front; she also had to carry a pair of scissors and a bottle of beer in her purse whenever she was out of the house; and a clerk carried a bottle of unused sedatives in his pocket for years, which acted as a magic talisman to him (Marks, 1978).

A tandem proved to be a vehicle to freedom for a Stockport housewife. Her husband watched for five years as she deteriorated from a happy-go-lucky person into a hysterical recluse. Trips in the car had failed to help her; she just hid under a blanket and screamed to go back home. He invested in two tandems, and with the help of the 'bicycle made for two' she slowly became mobile once more, going out on trips with her husband and two daughters. Her husband thought that the effort of cycling gave her less time to worry about her fears.

Most agoraphobia sufferers feel much safer in a car, and the lucky ones who can drive are capable of extending their range of activities far beyond the non-driver. On the other hand, I had been driving for ten years before I got agoraphobia, and I felt much worse in a car. The explanation for this apparent contradiction is simple: I felt trapped in a car. Most agoraphobia sufferers do not, and the car provides an excellent line of escape over a long distance, enabling them to extend their 'beat' over a far wider radius.

At times I could not tolerate Jim being in the car with me, and felt a great sense of relief when I drove on my own. Again, the reason for this is straightforward. As long as an agoraphobe feels in control of a situation, he will not get his symptoms. Without a companion, I felt I was in full control of the car, and I had no need to ask anyone if I wanted to stop, go home, or go somewhere else if I chose. I was constantly terrified of the demands that other people might make on me, because I felt I would probably not be able to cope with them. Having someone with me inevitably made extra demands, simply because another person had to be considered, and I felt I had enough problems of my own without the smallest addition from outside. I found it doubly difficult to be a passenger in a car for the same reasons, and for years it was impossible for me to travel with anyone but Jim.

In a way this particular agoraphobic quirk had its advantages. It meant I actually preferred to go out on my newspaper jobs on my own, but if a photographer was required to go along on the same job, he had to go in his own car.

My desire and preference for being on my own when going outside was also exceptional. Most agoraphobes prefer company and feel safer with someone else. I felt more trapped by being with other people, no matter how sympathetic.

The telephone is a great boon to agoraphobes because it helps to keep them in touch with the outside world. Being left on your own is a major fear for many sufferers, and the telephone can give the family more freedom, since the agoraphobe knows he can ring for help if he begins to get distressed. This can free a husband or wife to go out to work while leaving the agoraphobe at home.

The majority of agoraphobes derive great consolation and encouragement through belonging to groups and societies of other phobia sufferers, but a small percentage (which included myself) have no wish at all to meet other people in the same predicament. Hearing other tales of woe made me feel more depressed and facing people who had had agoraphobia for many decades tended to sap my courage and hope of a cure. My whole energies were directed to rejoining the land of the living, and being with other agoraphobes would have made me feel I belonged to some alien race in which I did not believe. The practice of herding together patients with kindred mental disorders can be completely misguided since it can reinforce feelings of isolation from the general community. I believe I got better a lot faster through always working and living within a normal environment, no matter how difficult it could be for me.

My desire to be alone and independent took almost contradictory forms as I began to get better. I needed Jim to get me to places further afield, but I disliked having to rely on him. On our first holiday while recovering, I was very excited by my achievement, yet very resentful that I had only managed it with Jim's help. Nevertheless, Jim's support was essential in the healing process.

Agoraphobia sufferers need true friends, because I doubt that any-one else could put up with them. (See p. 182.)

ANONYMITY

The urgent need for anonymity must hide many thousands of agoraphobes from the eye of the public. Women can have agora-phobia for many years without their neighbours guessing, and men will try even harder to mask their symptoms. The first, and sometimes the only, people to know of an agoraphobe is the person's immediate family, with the sufferer even refusing to tell his own doctor.

Although phobias, and agoraphobia in particular, are enjoying quite a vogue among writers and the media at the present time, a scan through the cuttings files of two major national newspapers produced less than 20 agoraphobia stories over a span of ten years —1969–79. *Daily Mail* staff reporter Ian Fletcher, who did the search, was convinced that some 'big names' would be found associated with the agoraphobia stories, but he reckoned without the agoraphobe's need for anonymity. It is hard enough for ordin-ary housewives to tell their horror stories to the newspapers: it is almost suicidal for someone who is prominent in society and try-ing to maintain a normal façade.

A notable exception is the wife of David Sheppard, the former England cricketer who is now Anglican Bishop of Liverpool. In 1975, Grace Sheppard bravely faced the television cameras to tell of her battle with agoraphobia. Accompanied by her husband on the BBC 1 programme *Anno Domini*, she described how her illness started when she was going for a train on London's Underground. She suddenly felt as though she could no longer breathe, and after-wards became truly agoraphobic, unable to go outside or do her shopping. As a bishop's wife, it was a terrible twist that agora-phobia prevented her for a time from entering a packed church.

Speaking to me in 1980 of her 23 years experience of agora-phobia Mrs Sheppard said: 'It was made increasingly difficult to keep my agoraphobia quiet by the media and in fact I was urged to explain why I "wouldn't" speak at meetings when we came up to Liverpool. Bishops's wives are necessarily very public and exposed!

'The programme I did with my husband four Christmasses ago remarkably is still having an impact on people. They write and ring. There are so many people with this distressing condition, and as you rightly say, anonymity is *very* important for so many sufferers. I've had people tell me they have not told a soul for 26 years for instance.'

Grace Sheppard has since made great strides in overcoming her agoraphobia facing and coping with her fears with a courage which all agoraphobes will know and appreciate.

She said: 'As you mention, it is a terrible twist to be the partner of such a public person. However, his accepting and supportive attitude helps me so much to set my targets higher at mostly my own pace. The support of husband, family and friends is crucial.

'Although I still suffer from this thing, I can drive around and shop alone, sit in services and big public occasions, and I even flew to Ireland alone to address a conference in Greystones for two days.

'Learning to say "No" is an important part while recognising that to withdraw completely would be a great mistake for me. It is fortunately not a strong temptation which I think indicates how much better I have become over the last 23 years. Agoraphobia does not make sense and yet maybe it keeps us humble,' she concluded.

The need for anonymity can sometimes be a practical necessity. Professor Leonard used all his social tactics to conceal his phobic condition because he believed that the university administration would have used the knowledge as the one decisive argument for his dismissal. He had reason to fear other people, for when his first wife Agatha committed suicide he was blamed for her death by his in-laws, friends and acquaintances. who socially ostracised him.

People in public life who are suffering from agoraphobia have little to gain from their condition becoming known. It should be remembered that membership of phobic societies is not just confined to housewives and ordinary working people, but includes people from all walks of life, including television newscasters, journalists, psychiatric nurses, teachers, ministers, bankers and many other professional people. My anonymity was very precious to me until I began to get on top of agoraphobia, and I am sure this is the case for most agoraphobes.

An agoraphobe who wishes to retain as normal an appearance as possible becomes an expert in manipulation. Children, husbands and wives are used to run errands outside the home, or are used as props when going out on a short journey. Mail order catalogues are indispensable for ordering clothes or larger items which would normally entail a journey into town. The excuses for not going out are legion, and are usually quite convincing to the outsider.

I shared the all-enveloping desire for no one to find out about my agoraphobia, a desire which was born of fear that people would not understand, would think me strange or even insane. Initially I suspected that my symptoms did show some form of severe mental illness, so there was no reason that I could see why the rest of the world should disagree with me.

Being fairly well known before becoming agoraphobic, trying to keep a low profile was probably more difficult for me than for the average sufferer. When fighting off my panic symptoms, the last thing I wanted was to be noticed, but all too often I would be ushered to a front seat when all I wanted was a seat at the back of a public room, and remarks would be addressed to me during meetings where reporters would normally be left strictly alone. On one memorable occasion my agoraphobia brought a complete district council meeting to a halt. As I crept out of the district council chamber, worn out by my raging symptoms, a councillor interrupted the agenda to 'thank the press before they leave for their very attractive appearance this evening'. Fortunately I never lost my sense of humour throughout my agoraphobia, and if these events did little for my paranoia, they invariably appealed to my sense of the ridiculous.

In fact, my fears of being unmasked proved groundless. Within the editorial office of the newspaper where I worked, it was six months before I was 'found out', and this was only because I had been requested to cover a job about 40 miles away. I went into the editor's office, heart pounding, and told him that I could not do the job because I had agoraphobia. He glanced up at me and said: 'That's interesting. Write a feature on it.' I did, and that was all there was to it.

As I improved, I began to lose all shame of being an agoraphobe, and regarded it as a disability which had to be put up with for the moment, like any other ailment. If people found out that I had agoraphobia and could not take it, that was their misfortune, not mine. However, the amount of ignorance on the subject did annoy me, and as I lost my fear of being an agoraphobe, so I lost any fear of discussing it. The reporter who trained me in journalism and who knew I was an agoraphobe moved on to Granada Television, from where I received an invitation in 1977 to talk in a series on phobias being presented by Daniel Topolski, Olympic rower and journalist. It took courage, because whereas before only a small number of people knew of my condition, now a great number were likely to find out.

The public reaction was tremendous. Many people knew me anyway as a journalist, archaeologist and antiques expert, but after the screening of the interview I found that landlords of pubs, restaurant owners and many other unlikely people were slapping me on the back and saying: 'Marvellous. I'd never have guessed. Well done!' I later did two 15-minute programmes on agoraphobia for Radio Blackburn, and again public and private reaction was very positive.

The reason for this is that because I accepted my agoraphobia and did not find it alarming or different, neither did the people who watched and listened. If I had spoken with any fear about my agoraphobia, I am sure other people would have reacted very differently.

This helps to explain the reaction to newspaper articles written by a Swansea agoraphobe, who had been given little understanding of her condition by psychiatrists, and who also had been told that she was incurable. The Welsh community in which she lived did not understand, thought agoraphobia was a mental disease, and subsequently gave the unfortunate woman a wide berth.

AGORAPHOBIA AND OUTSIDE INFLUENCES

Outside factors such as the weather, buildings and local scenery can affect agoraphobia quite dramatically. In the National Survey of Agoraphobics, 66 per cent said certain places in their neighbourhood made them feel worse, and 56 per cent said cloudy, depressing weather had the same effect (Burns and Thorpe, 1977b).

Not surprisingly, agoraphobes will dislike an area in direct relation to how high and wide the space encountered is likely to be. If there are objects to break up the scenery, such as alleyways, trees and bushes, the place becomes far more acceptable, since ways of escape and areas to rest the eyes are in immediate view. Like many agoraphobes, I preferred to move around at night, under cover of darkness. During the day sunglasses were a boon, since besides shielding me from the bright sunlight, they helped to hide my face and fears. I found windy weather particularly difficult to cope with since it is very 'feely'. With fear of feeling already rocketing inside me, the last thing I wanted was to sense the wind whipping my face and skin, and blowing through my hair and clothes.

Hot weather also can decrease the agoraphobe's resistance to his symptoms. During the big drought which afflicted Britain in 1976, the hot, dry days affected me badly; the heat intensified my fear of feeling and my fear of being trapped because I could not get away from it. Physically, it made me very breathless and uncomfortable, and I became less tolerant of any other stress or feeling which came my way. It is no great discovery that heat can raise the stress level in many individuals. In New York, for instance, the crime rate noticeably increases as temperatures get higher and tempers become more frayed.

I was frightened by any weather which might impede my way home—snow, fog and rain would encourage me to stay indoors.

But many agoraphobes find that rain actually helps them to go out, providing a natural cover for their fears, where they feel less conspicuous.

Those soft, balmy days full of sunshine and flowers, which occasionally occur during British summers, were very painful to me. Far from cheering me up, they merely acted as an all too brilliant reflector of the sad state of my own agoraphobic life. The freedom of the birds and insects, the distant shouts of children playing, the knowledge of the seaside only 10 miles distant, would nearly tear my heart out. I was much more emotionally in tune with the damp, dark drabness of a West Lancashire winter.

The period of my agoraphobia coincided with a period of great industrial unrest in England with strikes becoming a regular hazard of everyday living. In particular, I found electricity strikes in winter almost beyond my agoraphobic endurance, since they attacked in a very direct way my ultimate place of refuge. Already frozen with inner fear, the removal of heat and light by an untouchable outer force was quite terrifying.

Vincent found that ugly architecture intensified his fear. As one's toleration level is virtually nil when venturing out on any agoraphobic journey, the slightest thing, such as a personal revulsion to buildings, can push up the stress level to panic point. Vincent also remarked that darkness appeared to have a quietening effect on him, and storms and blizzards greatly alleviated his symptoms, probably because his view was obstructed. Similarly, he liked the waves to be rolling high when he went out in a boat, and dreaded calm waters. In effect, the outside storms and turmoil took his mind off, or found sympathy with, his own stormy interior, balancing the fear so that he could function more normally. He loved quiet wooded countryside with plenty of underbrush, and low hills and little valleys—landscape which was quiet and restful, where he could rest his eyes. Bold and rugged landscape could quickly reduce him to terror.

In almost all instances, the outside factors which can intensify agoraphobia are ones which intensify feeling beyond the person's toleration capacity. The outside factors which diminish agoraphobia are ones which help to bring down the tension level. Although the individuals' likes and dislikes will be as variable as themselves, the basic reasons for their reaction to outside factors will be the same.

Occasionally outside factors can intrude completely on agoraphobia such as wars, fires, earthquakes and other acts of God. The agoraphobe's reaction to these is straightforward. If the house is on fire, he gets out, or if bombs are dropping, he runs, regardless of his agoraphobia, but his symptoms will reassert themselves after the emergency.

In 1952, V. A. Kral noted that in the concentration camp of Theresienstadt in Nazi-occupied Europe, where the majority of inmates died or were sent to extermination camps, phobic symptoms either disappeared completely or disappeared to the extent that patients could work; but after some months of liberation, there was a tendency for the old symptoms to reassert themselves. Similarly, an agoraphobe who was forced to flee from Europe during the war managed the journey to the United States, and then reverted back to her previous housebound state.

It can be seen from this that traumatic outside events can provide sufficiently acute distraction to take the person's mind off their phobia, but once the stimulus is removed, the symptoms tend to come back as before.

Outside events may force an agoraphobe to leave the safety of home in less dramatic circumstances. In 1978, a 35-year-old man who had had agoraphobia for 20 years was required to appear in court. He had never stepped outside his mother's council flat since he was 15, so he was allowed to stand in a corridor leading from the jailer's office to the court-room, rather than face the ordeal of appearing in the dock in open court.

The same year, a Scottish housewife was treated even more mercifully by a local magistrate. When it was learned that she was unable to attend court because of agoraphobia, the magistrate arranged for the court to be held in the living room of her council house. The mother of four was charged with failing to send her eight-year-old son to school, but when the family problems were discovered—she could not even get to the doctor—she escaped with a warning, and was thanked by the magistrate for making the court, complete with assessor, fiscal, clerk and policemen, welcome in her home.

Finally, a word about the hopeless cases—the agoraphobes who prefer their affliction to any cure. Unbelievably, these people do exist, since life for them would be more intolerable without their agoraphobia. Sometimes a shaky marriage can be held together permanently by agoraphobia, since the non-agoraphobic partner's continual presence and support seems absolutely essential. If a woman knows that the disappearance of her agoraphobia will in all likelihood lead to the disappearance of her husband, since he is no longer needed, she is unlikely to throw away the security of her position by getting better.

Agoraphobia can be a convenient, if drastic excuse not to take on a new job or responsibilities. It also can be used as blackmail to ensure the devotion of people around you. Agoraphobia makes sure you are the centre of attention in the family whether you like it or not, and some emotionally inadequate people would find they had no limelight in life at all without it.

The chances of curing such people from agoraphobia are slim indeed since the secondary gains are such that there is no real motivation to get better. I am well aware that this book will be unwelcome and no doubt ignored by the committed agoraphobe, who will already have successfully ignored or refused all other forms of help as too difficult or too hard. It will be doubly unwelcome since there are now very concrete moves one can take to get rid of the condition.

On the other hand, I trust my book will be welcomed by the vast majority of agoraphobia sufferers who have the urgent will and need to get better, and by their families and friends who equally wish them health and happiness.

REFERENCES

Burns, L. E. and Thorpe, G. L. (1977a). Fears and Clinical Phobias: Epidemiological Aspects and the National Survey of Agoraphobics. *Journal of International Medical Research*, 5 (1), 137.

Burns, L. E. and Thorpe, G. L. (1977b). The Epidemiology of Fears and Phobias (With Particular Reference to the National Survey of Agoraphobics). *Journal of International Medical Research*, 5 (5), 5.

Kral, V. A. (1952). Psychiatric Observations under Severe Chronic Stress. *American Journal of Psychiatry*, 108, 105.

Marks, Isaac M. (1978). *Living with Fear. Understanding and Coping with Anxiety*, p. 87–88. McGraw-Hill Book Company, London and New York.

Mullaney, J. A. and Trippett, C. J. (1979). Alcohol Dependence and Phobias: Clinical Description and Relevance. *British Journal of Psychiatry*, 135, 565–573.

Westphal, C. (1871–2). Die Agoraphobie: Eine Neuropathische Erscheinung. *Archiv für Psychiatrie und Nervenkrankheiten*, 3, 138–171, 219–221.

Chapter 5

Treatment—The Orthodox Approach

My battle back to health started in a cabbage field. After giving up my museum job I had to find something to give me back a little self-respect and also to build me up physically, so I became a farm-worker.

I managed the quarter of an hour's drive to my parents' farm each day and did everything from cutting greens and spreading manure to tractor work and loading lorries. The fresh air, smell of the soil and lack of professional stress had its effects. I put on weight and muscle and became physically fitter than I had been for years. At the same time my agoraphobia got worse. The drive to work did not get any easier, and I could be housebound at any time. The minor tranquillisers which I was taking made no perceptible difference.

My refusal to take major tranquillisers was not based on ignorance or fear of the unknown but on previous experience prior to having agoraphobia. There have been recent suggestions that agoraphobia is often linked with people who have previously suffered from primary affective (emotional) disorders, and this may well be the case. Agoraphobia is a symptom of underlying physical and emotional problems, and these disorders can manifest themselves in many other ways before finally appearing in their most vicious form as agoraphobia.

In retrospect, I can see that agoraphobia was a logical conclusion to my previous life pattern. I was a sickly baby, having pneumonia three times, as well as all the other childhood ailments, and as a result I had to learn to walk three times. At five years old I got scarlet fever. A black van came for me in the night and took me to hospital where I was kept in isolation for some weeks. Unfortunately no one bothered to tell me where I was, why I was there or why my parents had apparently deserted me. I soon learned in my new 'home' that you were much more popular with the nurses if you did not cry, so I stopped crying for my parents. The net result of this traumatic experience was that when my father and mother were finally allowed in to see me, I did not recognise them, and I had to learn to walk again for the last time.

Predictably I suffered from nightmares and separation anxiety after this. I was acutely hypersensitive, my physical coordination was bad, and I tended to be a loner, avoiding group situations where I would get hurt. My eyesight began to deteriorate as school work got harder and I became very myopic.

Unexpectedly, I got my scholarship examination a year early, so I was sent to boarding school at the age of 10 and suffered badly from homesickness and a continuing inability to mix generally with the other pupils. A strict Catholic and isolated country up-bringing followed by seven years in a convent boarding school left me completely unprepared for the social and other pressures of going to university. Once there I tried to do too much, particularly on the social side, and by my second university year I began to get my first nervous symptoms, finally culminating in a complete in-ability to read.

The drugs prescribed by my doctor made me feel dreadful, and depression and desperation moved in as my examinations for that year approached. The psychiatrist to whom I had been referred suggested that I go as a voluntary patient to hospital, and there I received the biggest fright of my life when I discovered what psychiatric treatment then entailed.

A padded cell existed in the psychiatric ward and was in use while I was there, and the screams of the woman inside did nothing for the nerves of the rest of the inmates. The patients who I met were in a constant state of fear, and I soon learned that a 'good' psychiatric patient must never show any aggression, natural or unnatural, that you must never tell the psychiatrist how you really feel (that was asking for trouble), but always what he wants to hear, in order to get out with a clean bill of health.

After a week in that appalling place, I left and tried a second hospital where a more enlightened approach was taken. I was put on various drugs with side-effects ranging from nausea to total collapse, until one was found which 'suited' me. This was trifluoperazine (Stelazine), a major tranquilliser which is used to treat schizophrenia, paranoid delusional states, manic-depressive psychoses and delirium tremens. The doctors never told me what was the matter with me and I suspected they did not know, but finally they stated that I must do nothing more stimulating than cutting cabbages or the equivalent for the rest of my life, or they would not answer for the consequences. They were adamant that I must not return to university.

Stupefied with a maximum dose of drugs and told by the experts that this was the end of the line as far as any demanding or creative brain-work was concerned, I still could not face giving up everything I wanted in life. With the support of my parents, the university and eventually my specialist, I sat my examinations on my own in the summer vacation and passed, took a year's sabbatical leave, and returned to take my finals. It was a marvellous moment for me when I walked up to receive my honours degree from the Vice-Chancellor, even with the knowledge that the maximum I could read was still just three sides of a page per day.

I applied for and got my museum job, and I gradually worked at coming off the drugs to which I was firmly hooked by this time. It took three years, with a lot of withdrawal symptoms, but in the end I managed it. And within a year my agoraphobic symptoms started.

From this, it can be seen why I was less than enthusiastic about going back on major tranquillisers. In all fairness, the psychiatrists could claim some success for the drug treatment in that perhaps trifluoperazine, added to my own will to survive, got me as far as it did; and coming off the drug triggered off an equally serious if different set of symptoms.

What stuck out like a sore thumb in my mind was the fact that five years of drugs had done nothing to remove the cause of my various symptoms and I was just as vulnerable as before. Taking the drugs meant that I was living a half-life since I was unable to feel properly, but I could function to a limited extent. Once off the drugs, I was back in touch with my own feelings and had no barrier against outside events. As I was in an exciting and demand-ing job, it was inevitable that any extra stress was going to cause trouble and the logical thing happened.

Brought to my knees again by agoraphobia, I felt that the psy-chiatrists were vindicated in their original opinion. Perhaps if I cut cabbages for the rest of my life (and in no way was I comparing myself with the modern skilled farmworker), I would then be all right.

I did manage to achieve a superficial peace on the farm, but underneath I was a very unhappy person. Somehow my body and mind could never keep up with what I wanted to do. Professionally I knew I was a very capable person, but there seemed to be some kind of 'fatal flaw' in my make-up which failed me whatever I tried to do. I could not face going back on to major tranquillisers with all that entailed, nor was I prepared to put myself back into the hands of the psychiatric profession in which rightly or wrongly I had no confidence. It appeared at the time that I had reached the final impasse, with no way out whichever way I turned.

My psychiatric experience was an unfortunate one and should not be taken as typical. Happily, techniques and therapies have since improved and orthodox medicine has several avenues of treat-ment open to the agoraphobe.

THE GENERAL PRACTITIONER

The first person from whom an agoraphobe is likely to seek help is his own doctor. A good GP can make an enormous amount of difference to the agoraphobe by explaining the condition, removing fears of insanity, and giving sensible advice and treatment. Un-fortunately, this does not always happen since the doctor himself may not understand agoraphobia.

Medical reaction to agoraphobes can sometimes be very distressing as the following comments illustrate:

'I have had practically no help from GPs. In fact one was cruel enough to strike me from his list while I was going through a very depressive period and called him in to visit me. What else could I do? I now have a new GP who is kind and helpful, also I have a visit to a psychiatrist, but only every four months and I have to get someone to take me.'

'I cannot receive any treatment because the doctor will not refer me or even give me the drugs my last doctor gave me. I feel bitter because if I was a drop-out, somebody—i.e. the state—would help me. I get no financial assistance because I am not officially sick and yet I am not available for work. I feel that I am too normal to receive treatment, yet not normal enough to lead a relaxed life.'

'We are completely abandoned, prisoners in our own homes. It makes me so mad when I read of people in jail for crimes, getting every help and medical attention, and yet we have done no harm to anybody and are prisoners without help or sympathy.'

GPs who take a little time to listen and dispel fears are worth their weight in gold. As one Sussex mother put it: 'I asked my doctor if I was just being silly and should I fight my feelings and make myself do things. He said, "No, you will only make yourself worse. Try and go along with it instead, accept it because this is the way you are, and after a time you may find you can look it in the face and you will feel better." So, feeling not so insane as I had previously, I decided to do just that.'

If the patient is depressed, the doctor's first move will be to prescribe a tricyclic or monoamine oxidase inhibiting anti-depressant for several months. In addition he can encourage the patient to carry out exposure exercises, gradually bringing him to face and tolerate his fears without the aid of a therapist. It is important that the exposure programmes are well structured and systematic to be successful, and Isaac Marks' simple manual to help doctors, patients and relatives can form a useful baseline (Marks, 1978). The doctor can explain the programme to the patient and a relative or friend who will support and work with him for as long as it takes. The patient can set himself limited goals and re-enter phobic situations until anxiety begins to decrease, keeping a diary of his experiences as he does so. Progress and future goals can be worked out with the relative or friend, or with the doctor if necessary.

For many agoraphobes, simple advice from the doctor coupled with this self-help exposure programme will be sufficient to help them cope with panic to some extent, and to lead a more normal existence. Initially, some agoraphobes will need the help of a therapist to get through the feared situations; this can be a nurse, a psychologist or even an ex-phobic patient who understands the condition. Nurse-therapists have been used very effectively in helping agoraphobes in their own homes and are being used increasingly to help hospital outpatients and day patients. For instance, London's Maudsley Hospital trains nurses to administer psychological treatments.

This is the ideal reaction from the doctor, yet my sympathy goes out to GPs confronted with agoraphobic patients, whom they scarcely have the time or often the specialised knowledge to help. The psychosomatic illnesses so often associated with agoraphobia can easily be misinterpreted as hypochondria, and with little more than four or five minutes to spare per patient, the hard-pressed GP may feel he can do little or nothing for such a complicated and often exasperating condition.

Just the same, it can be seen that for a small investment in time, the GP can make a significant contribution towards helping his agoraphobic patient, both emotionally and practically, to cope more effectively with day-to-day living.

DRUG TREATMENT

The vast majority of agoraphobes receive drug treatment even though its success rate is very low. (See p. 184.) Anti-depressant drugs are used where appropriate, common ones in use being the tricyclic imipramine (Tofranil), the monoamine oxidase inhibitors phenelzine (Nardil) and isocarboxazid (Marplan) and iproniazid, which have proved effective only in the short-term.

Many papers have been published on the effects of drugs on agoraphobes, and on the whole the results have scarcely been impressive. In most cases the effects of anti-depressants are limited and take more than four weeks to emerge, the patients usually relapse once taken off the drugs, and the long-term effects are not known. It is still not clear whether anti-depressants simply reduce depression or act on the phobia when they are effective.

Clomipramine (Anafranil) was heralded as something of a 'miracle' drug when pilot studies in the 1970s indicated significant improvement in phobias after treatment. Subsequent research has reduced the enthusiasm, since the drug is only useful where the patient has depression, with a high relapse rate once the drug is stopped.

Drugs other than anti-depressants have also proved disappointing in treating phobic avoidance, including diazepam (Valium), intravenous thiopentone, and beta-blockers such as oxprenolol, alprenolol and propranolol. Large doses of sedatives such as amylobarbitone (Sodium Amytal) appear to have an adverse effect on exposure treatments, so patients have to be weaned off them before they are given any behavioural therapy. Anti-depressants do not affect behavioural therapy and can be used in conjunction with it (*Lancet*, 1979).

Side-effects from drugs also limit their use. In one trial testing of clomipramine on over 750 agoraphobic patients, 139 withdrew because of side-effects (Beaumont, 1977). Unwanted effects from this one drug include dry mouth, blurred vision, constipation, sweating, disturbance in passing urine, tremor and ataxia (defective control of muscles), hypotension, headaches, insomnia and, rarely, fits. Agoraphobes should make sure they know the possible side-effects of any drug they are prescribed so they do not confuse the artificial symptoms with their agoraphobia, thus adding to their anxiety.

In practice, drug therapy appears to be a rather hit-and-miss affair. A sufferer from Gwent tells a cautionary tale of how things can go wrong. She said: 'My husband took me to the doctor who said I was neurotic and put me on chlordiazepoxide (Librium). I found it made me depressed so he put me on diazepam (Valium). After two and a half years on this I had stepped up the dose so that if I *had* to go somewhere, I would take a handful and arrive drugged and ill and sit near the door ready to make a dash for it.

'In the summer I suddenly knew it could not go on. I was living in a twilight world because of too much diazepam, and yet I *still* had the panic bouts. Also the drugs took away any fight or resistance I might have had. I stopped taking all drugs, and a day later I collapsed. I had come off too quickly and was violently ill for two weeks.

'The doctor urged me to take diazepam again, but I wouldn't. I was obsessive about it. I felt I had to stay off them to survive. My tongue and oesophagus were permanently ulcerated, and swallowing or talking was difficult. I begged to see a psychiatrist, but was told that I was too intelligent to need one and that anyway psychiatrists had the highest suicide rate in the country.'

Despite this fatuous advice, she was eventually admitted to a psychiatric hospital for 10 days where the specialist told her that she had no recognisable mental illness. He told her that it could be a hysterical condition and she would just have to go home and wait. After nearly three years of treatment this woman was still entirely unaware that she had agoraphobia, and so it would seem were her doctors.

A Blackpool agoraphobe told a typical story of how she had been treated with more drugs than she could remember, but apart from chlordiazepoxide (Librium) which helped to calm her, the drugs were 'useless' and did not stop her panics. She said: 'I feel that not enough is done to help people with phobias. It's tablets and talk yourself out of it.'

Undoubtedly chemotherapy (drug treatment) has a part to play in the cure and control of agoraphobia, in so far as it helps to lower and stabilise the stress or tension level in the patient. Anything which helps to keep the stress level below panic point is useful, but the severe limitations of drugs in achieving this have to be recognised.

On the other hand I found sleeping tablets quite essential for getting better since they gave me a most necessary temporary respite from my symptoms during the night. When my agoraphobia was at its worst, I was lucky if I got four hours' sleep in as many days.

For a fortunate few, drugs have proved completely successful in combating agoraphobic symptoms but there probably will always be a nagging doubt in the person's mind whether the agoraphobia will appear again like a bolt from the blue. Once the artificial crutch of drugs is removed, the person is again reliant on his own emotional and physical resources to combat stress. If the underlying causes of his condition have not been resolved, the chances are that panic may strike again if he meets an extra stressful situation.

Another criticism of drugs is that once an agoraphobe becomes dependent on them, it becomes doubly difficult to manage without their support. A 32-year-old Manchester state registered nurse who suffered badly from agoraphobia said: 'The doctor gave me diazepam (Valium) and I coped on these for two years in full-time employment. When one day I went for some more diazepam he refused me, and I knew I could not cope without them. I came home from work that night and wanted to die. I knew I would never go out again.'

She eventually went to see a psychiatrist who put her on clomipramine (Anafranil), which made her feel she was dying. After diagnosing agoraphobia, he sent her to see a psychologist who took her off the clomipramine and gave her some relaxation exercises.

She was put on lorazepam (Ativan), but after months of treatment there was no improvement in her symptoms.

Small wonder that less than 17 per cent of agoraphobes in the National Survey found tablets and medicine useful, and high time indeed that doctors stopped doling out millions of expensive tranquillisers and anti-depressants in the hope that they will cure agoraphobia. Nine times out of ten, they won't.

Agoraphobes themselves have probably contributed to the popularity of chemotherapy, since in our 'pill for every ill' society they would undoubtedly feel aggrieved if they did not come out of the doctor's surgery clutching a prescription.

In practical terms, the average doctor simply has not got the time to deal with the real causes of agoraphobia or other nervous disorders, which often make up half a doctor's workload. Sadly, often all he can do is use drugs to damp down stress symptoms and give the nervous system a chance to recuperate, hoping in the meantime that the cause may right itself naturally.

THE BEHAVIOURAL APPROACH

One of the most significant advances in the treatment of agoraphobia during the past decade has been the development of exposure or behavioural techniques. The sufferer is brought face to face with his fears, either in imagination or reality, and is left 'exposed' to them for fairly long periods until his panic lessens and finally dies away. This controlled exposure will gradually desensitise the agoraphobe, bringing down the panic threshold until, it is hoped, it no longer exists.

Behaviourists differ fundamentally from other therapists, since they have no interest in underlying psychological causes but seek only to change behaviour patterns. In their opinion the agoraphobe has learnt to react wrongly to certain stimuli, so must be retrained to react correctly and without fear.

The most usual behavioural techniques used for agoraphobia include:

desensitisation: the patient is exposed very gently to the feared situation

flooding: the sufferer is thrown in at the deep end and exposed immediately and completely to his greatest fear

implosion: patients are asked to imagine themselves in their most frightening situation for an hour or more with the assistance of the therapist

exposure in phantasy: the assistance of films and slides of the feared situation are used

modelling: the therapist acts as a model for the patient

shaping: the therapist encourages the patient to confront the phobic situation with him

operant conditioning: the patient is rewarded when he succeeds in overcoming a difficulty

simple relaxation.

Isaac Marks has claimed that three-quarters of cooperative patients can be restored to normal functioning through this treatment. He states that by using steady exposure to the frightening situation, agoraphobes can usually improve within 10 one-hour sessions. Phobias which have been present for 20 years have been overcome in three hours of therapy, although 10 to 20 hours are usually necessary in one- or two-hour sessions to eliminate the fears (Marks, 1978).

Other doctors have formed a less favourable impression of behavioural therapy, with agoraphobes showing a limited response, improvement occurring only during treatment and no further gains being made during the follow-up period. Methods of measuring improvement in phobias also tend to vary between researchers and some rationalisation is necessary if results are to be fully meaningful.

It has been found that there is little difference in the long-term between exposing patients to real or imagined phobic situations, as long as they are encouraged to practice between sessions.

Group therapy is favoured by many hospitals and is popular because of the obvious economic advantages, but generally it does not lead to continuing improvement once patients have completed the therapists' programme.

A home-treatment programme developed at Warneford Hospital, Oxford, showed that it produced at least equivalent results to clinic-based treatment and three-quarters of the patients went on to make further behavioural gains during a follow-up period (Mathews et al, 1977).

According to the National Survey, behavioural therapy is the most effective of all treatments for agoraphobia, but, even so, the results are poor—only a little above 30 per cent of those surveyed had found it very helpful. (See p. 184.) The phobic societies in general are not impressed with exposure techniques, with one organiser stating that one had only to read the 50 or 60 letters she got per day to know how unsuccessful are such therapies.

A Gloucestershire agoraphobe gave a good example of why behavioural therapy was ultimately ineffective for him. He was invited to volunteer as a research subject at the newly established Psychological Treatment Research Unit at Oxford, where he was treated with desensitisation and flooding by one of the researchers.

He said: 'Together we did all sorts of hair-raising things: revisiting all the places in Oxford; diving into the basement of Marks and Spencer (no windows at all); pushing through the crowds at St Giles' Fair. I did it all, shattered but euphoric; but what I could not do was to reproduce the same kind of exploits *here*. The researcher even came over one day and I went through all the hoops here; but always with the knowledge that I should not be able to do it on my own next day—even though part of the treatment always was to be sent off alone into all the worst situations. In the end I reluctantly resigned.'

On the whole it would seem that once behavioural therapy stops, improvement does not necessarily continue but stays at the same level, or even diminishes once treatment is concluded.

Nevertheless behavioural therapy remains one of the most attractive treatments since it is something concrete which can be tackled positively by both patient and doctor. Results are self-evident and some progress either small or sometimes spectacular can usually be expected. Even if improvement does not necessarily continue after treatment, at least some headway has been made in coping with the dreadful symptoms.

Agoraphobes who are rather less motivated to get better, or who are worn down by their suffering, will benefit from the discipline of a structured behavioural programme laid down by a therapist who is there to see it carried through.

Behavioural therapy can sometimes amount to a virtual cure if the body and mind have been brought to face panic and have been taught to live through it, so relieving the agoraphobic symptoms by bringing down the tension level to manageable proportions. With sufficient will power on the part of the agoraphobe, and skilled and patient management on the part of the doctor, wonders can indeed be achieved without bothering to delve into any underlying cause of the agoraphobia.

Indeed, whatever the criticism of behavioural techniques, every agoraphobe has to face the fact that his recovery must at some point include exposure to the feared situation. There is no way round it and no easy way out. Panic and fear have to be faced head on, time and time again, until they no longer have the power to keep him housebound or limited in his existence. Whatever therapy the agoraphobe is undergoing and no matter how effective it is proving, the effort of getting out of the house has always to be made, and if there is a structured programme and therapist to help him that is very much in his favour.

I got my behavioural therapy in the natural run of things, first by travelling to see my therapist. As I set off in my car each time every fibre in my being was screaming: 'I can't do it! I can't do it!' and I still thought I couldn't do it when I got there. The journey to see the therapist, which I accomplished every week for years, never got any easier until I was really better. This was because it was of paramount importance to me to get there, and the consequent pressure and fear of not managing it—and I knew I would miss my appointment if I was late— made sure I was very agoraphobic on the way there, but rarely agoraphobic on the way home. Being a journalist was also magnificent exposure treatment, since I was forced to go into the most feared public situations every day while also coping with the normal cut and thrust of the job.

I found that where behavioural therapy can go wrong is in the belief that by doing things over and over again they will of necessity become easier in the long run. On its own there is very little curative value and sometimes positive harm in forcing yourself out into situations you fear. The secret is that it is not what you do that counts, but how you do it.

The following are good examples of how an agoraphobe should not attempt to go outside: they relate to the very last attempts I made to lead a normal life before giving into my symptoms. After leaving the museum I managed to go on a week's archaeological excavation in Greater Manchester, staying at a hall of residence, and I went to visit a friend who ran a museum in the West Midlands. I also went on a day's shopping trip to London, which included a bomb scare on the train at Crewe. These trips did not make me feel any better, but actually made me worse because they made no difference at all to my problems. The same journeys would be just as hard the next time, and I knew it.

The reason why the trips had an adverse effect was because my main motive was to prove to myself and everyone else that I was still normal. Obviously panic attacks and fears were not in my agenda, and when they happened, as they certainly did under my self-induced pressure, they reinforced my fears alarmingly, so that I did not bother trying to get away from my local area again for years.

Under those sort of conditions an agoraphobe could go to Timbuktu and back again every day of the week and still be worse at the end of it. Conversely, if he made one five-minute journey per week in the right way and for the right reasons, improvement would immediately begin to happen.

The right way means first, accepting that you are an agoraphobe; second, accepting your fears in a thoroughly realistic way; and third, working your way through them until you get used to them to the point where they begin to disappear for good. The healing process has started once you start walking right through the middle of your terror, again and again until it no longer affects you.

Practical behavioural advice is of paramount importance to the agoraphobe. Faced with a blanket refusal to go out, the doctor or therapist should start looking for chinks in the patient's armour. When my therapist asked me of what I was most frightened, with great difficulty I finally managed to tell him that if I panicked and did not find a lavatory, I was scared of dirtying myself. From this, he showed me how foolish my inhibitions were about using toilets in public houses, hotels, garages and restaurants at will, and even dashing behind a convenient bush when necessary.

Jim helped me over this particular problem in a very practical manner my flinging me bodily over a hedgerow into a field on one very panicky journey. Turning a singularly deaf ear to my maidenly entreaties and embarrassment until I had relieved myself, he only then allowed me back into the car. Looking back I can laugh at my antics, but at the time I felt I had climbed a small Mount Everest.

Occasionally doctors can show an amazing lack of common sense in advising their agoraphobic patients. Joy Melville tells a horrific story of a young man in New York who admitted to the same fear of incontinence which affected me and affects millions of people to a greater or lesser degree. His psychiatrist suggested that he went out and wet himself in public to get over his fear. The man tried it on the beach with the very natural result that he felt ashamed, and it did not cure him (Melville, 1977).

There is no skill in demonstrating to people that they can wet their pants in public—that is learning to lose control completely unconstructively. There is a great deal of skill in showing them step by step that they never need to wet themselves because there is always a way out. Having a Rolls-Royce with a built-in lavatory or sitting on a bucket in a second-hand car does help some agoraphobes to get about more easily, but it is hardly the complete answer. The answer lies in not being afraid of the natural reactions of your body and being thoroughly practical in your approach to your problems.

A rich Swiss businessman suffered badly from mikrophobia (fear of germs) as well as agoraphobia and could not tolerate the thought of going into public lavatories if he panicked. To get over this hurdle, his therapist suggested that he used the superior facilities provided by the best hotels in whatever part of town he was in at the time. Big hotels are hardly likely to do spot checks on who uses their toilets, and this simple practical advice helped the businessman on the way to resuming a normal life.

When I was persuaded to think what would actually happen if I lost control in a public meeting, I realised the worst possible events would be fainting, being sick or running to the lavatory, and the most extreme negative reactions I would be likely to encounter would be total indifference or one or two curious glances. By being encouraged to judge the reality of my fears in this way, it made it easier to actually go out and face them. I began to accept how dreadful I could feel on social and professional occasions, and knowing the terror could strike did not stop me from going out.

The agoraphobe should realise that the first time he is terrified by panic and stays wherever he is, seeing it through to the other side, is the most important moment of his life. From then on it is a downhill ride all the way, because nothing will ever be harder than what he has already so bravely achieved.

Once the healing process was underway I found that I could go for longer and longer periods without getting agoraphobic symptoms. Then suddenly the panic would leap on me again out of the blue, seeming doubly terrifying, shocking and painful because of its previous absence. This is an illusion which should be welcomed and understood by the agoraphobe since it is proof he is getting better.

It was as if I consistently reached a higher toleration level every time I faced my fear and worked my way through it to the exhausted calm on the other side. It is a savage process to go through, but the person who comes out at the end of it will have the inner strength and resilience of the most highly tempered steel, a marvellous attribute to take with you into the future.

As I steadily exposed myself to my fears and my toleration

improved, it became increasingly obvious that I could always get to events which I wanted to attend, but if I was invited somewhere and my heart was not in it, I promptly got all my agoraphobic symptoms and had to stay in. Whether I liked it or not, my condition forced absolute personal honesty on me. In the end, I realised the hopelessness of going against what my inner self was telling me—it just made me ill—and I no longer attempted to see people or go to places in which I had little or no genuine interest. Superficial but strong social pressures simply went to the wall for good, and I found a new freedom in being myself rather than the social hypocrite of the past.

Behavioural therapy on its own would never have cured my agoraphobia, but I recognise that it would have assisted me in coping with my symptoms. Behaviourists have made a most valuable contribution towards the management of agoraphobia, but their approach is more an added weapon in the armoury for combating agoraphobic symptoms than the ultimate answer to the problem.

ELECTRO-CONVULSIVE THERAPY

Severe agoraphobia cases may be treated with electro-convulsive therapy (ECT), especially if clinical depression is also present. ECT or EST (electro-shock therapy), as it is also known, has become something of a bogey in the public eye, despite its use in psychiatric medicine for over 35 years. The adverse publicity which it has received is probably because it has become increasingly clear that doctors and psychiatrists know nothing about the way ECT actually relieves depression. There is also a natural human revulsion to the idea that a 'fit' is to be artificially induced by passing an electric current through the brain under anaesthesia.

On the other hand, the anti-ECT lobby which has successfully curtailed its use in some states of the USA has possibly over-reacted to a therapy which has helped some patients where other therapies have failed. As most fear is born of ignorance, a brief description of what actually happens with ECT will not be out of place here.

Ideally, the patient is fully informed of what the treatment entails, so most fears can be allayed beforehand. Items such as dentures, jewellery, and hairclips are removed, and the patient, who has not eaten or drunk since midnight, is asked to empty his bladder and bowels prior to premedication. Two drugs are administered, probably by injection in the arm, one to put him to sleep and the other to relax his muscles. Saline-pad electrodes are placed bilaterally or unilaterally on the patient's temples and a small electric current lasting less than one second is passed through the brain while the patient is anaesthetised. The relaxing drug prevents a fully-fledged fit since the muscles are prevented from moving, and the nurse is ready to prevent any injury to the patient.

The convulsion causes a discharge of current by the brain cells. Despite the mystery surrounding ECT it is known that any subsequent improvement in mood is related to whether or not a fit was induced and not to the amount of electrical current used. A course of six to 12 sessions is normally used, depending on the result. Complications which ECT can cause are headaches, memory loss, temporary confusion and lack of concentration.

An Aberdare man who has suffered from agoraphobia for 30 years gave his own description of the benefits and drawbacks of ECT: 'The hospital treatment which did improve me for several years was at first the drastic one of ECT which cleared a lot of my depression etc but later affected my memory and concentration, and sometimes I cannot recall events of years ago which my family talk about. I have fairly good intelligence and have had scores of letters and some articles and one short story published in the national and local periodicals, though not so often lately owing to lack of concentration after ECT treatment, which I would advise phobic patients to avoid if possible.'

Despite considerable improvement after two periods of hospital treatment and managing to keep in work from 1955 to 1970, his improvement lessened with a subsequent decade of unemployment and a re-emergence of his symptoms.

On the whole, trained hypnotherapists will refuse to use hypnosis on any client who has had ECT within the past six months since an 'electrical brain storm' (technically an extreme abreactive myoclonic spasm) can be triggered off by this form of deep relaxation. Arthur Janov, one of the most controversial psychologists in the USA and originator of 'primal' therapy, has found that when his patients relive the trauma of their shock treatment the released pain is very great. (Janov believes all neuroses stem from the primal (infant) pains which are felt but never expressed.)

If ECT does work, the patient is handicapped by not knowing how, and possibly will not have the confidence of someone who has faced and worked through his fears and who knows that he can cope if his panic does return for a while.

ECT would seem only to have something to offer the more severe forms of agoraphobia and depression. Its 'unknown quantity' and possible side-effects should limit its use to all but a few sufferers, and then it should only be used as a last resort.

PSYCHOSURGERY

In extreme cases of agoraphobia a modified form of brain surgery may be used, but this is a comparatively rare occurrence, with probably less than 100 such operations for anxiety states taking place in Britain each year. Like ECT, psychosurgery has received a bad press, largely due to the early operations in the 1940s where the surgery could result in undesirable personality changes. Leucotomy (or lobotomy, as the surgical techniques for anxiety are called in the USA) has since been refined and modified so there is less danger of unwanted side-effects from destroyed brain tissue. The operation originally consisted of the destruction of a small part of the white matter in the frontal lobes of the brain. Modern operations consist of implanting small radioactive pellets so that a very small part of the frontal lobe or other special areas in the brain are irradiated.

Modified leucotomy is possibly justified for severely disabled patients who have failed to respond to any other treatment. However, in the light of recent developments (see Chapters 7 and 8) it must be viewed with extreme caution.

PSYCHOTHERAPY

Individual or group psychotherapy is being viewed increasingly as an adjunctive rather than a primary therapy for agoraphobia, with behavioural techniques taking precedence. However, Isaac Marks's opinion is that psychological treatments offer the most hope for lasting improvement for phobia sufferers, unless marked depression is also present (Marks, 1978). Simply talking of one's fears to an attentive and understanding listener can make a great deal of difference to an agoraphobia sufferer. Going deeper and trying to find the underlying or subconscious sources for the symptoms of agoraphobia can be of great benefit to the sufferer in helping him to understand why his strange fears have come about.

The obvious handicap of psychotherapy is that it is very expensive and can take years to complete, and unless an agoraphobe is prepared to pay privately for a course of psychotherapy it is unlikely that he will get it in any substantial form on the British National Health Service.

A Gloucestershire agoraphobe gave his explanation for psychotherapy having such a poor record in phobic conditions. 'The reason is because the average NHS psychiatrist is totally unanalysed and adopts an eclectic approach, based upon his own unconscious problems, which he inevitably projects upon his unfortunate patient,' he claimed. (See p. 184.)

If the origins of agoraphobia can be traced to incidents in the past history of the sufferer, this does not mean that cure will automatically follow. What psychotherapy can do is give the patient understanding of his present reactions in the light of the past, and from there the patient has something concrete to tackle, resulting in an improved life pattern.

Psychotherapy formed the major part of my treatment for over four years, and, with or without agoraphobia, it was a fascinating experience. It was also extremely painful in emotional terms, which may put off some people from going through with it, since the process of cure may be more painful than the actual condition. The terror of psychotherapy is in seeing yourself as you really are instead of what you think you are or ought to be, and it can accurately be equated with the horror of Oscar Wilde's Dorian Gray when he was confronted with the portrait which gave away his real and unacceptable personality (*The Picture of Dorian Gray*, 1891).

Like many people, I initially regarded psychotherapy with great suspicion and I did not relish the thought of 'lying on a couch and talking about sex'. In fact I did not have to lie on a couch, and the therapist rarely told me what he thought but helped me to find out what I really felt, which was a much more hair-raising experience. Psychotherapy helped me to see the emotional origins of my fears, and by a thorough emotional catharsis got rid of feelings blocked up in the past. It gave me the gift of knowing why I needed agoraphobia to keep me in the house. Deep down, I was terrified of people and a strict religious upbringing and years in a convent boarding school had given me enough sexual hang-ups to sink a battleship. I had so much suppressed aggression that I would grind pieces out of my teeth while sleeping, and the effort of trying to please everyone all of the time was impossible to maintain. Stripped to the foundations of my inner being, I had to stagger along the stony road of 'growing up' at the grand old age of 30 years.

Theoretically, once a person's real fears have been unearthed and he has come to terms with them, his agoraphobic symptoms should vanish since there is no further use for them : the fear of fear has been removed. This does happen for agoraphobes whose problems are purely emotionally based. For myself it began to happen, but only up to the stage where I could cope, very painfully, with holding down a newspaper job and leading a limited social life at home. Life was much richer than ever before but I was certainly not cured : the answer was to lie elsewhere. I doubt if I could ever have gone through the pain of psychotherapy unless I had been driven into a desperate agoraphobic corner, but I gained the very precious prize of knowing and liking myself after 30 years of running away from the 'real me'.

The expense, the long treatment and the emotional suffering of psychotherapy will naturally minimise its application to the agoraphobic population, but for those who do go through with it, there are very deep benefits, if not always a total cure. Without the background of my psychotherapeutic treatment, my final cure would not have been so complete, and for agoraphobes with a purely emotional basis for their condition, psychotherapy can result in full recovery. (See pp. 158–60.)

HYPNOTISM

Hypnotism was first accepted as a valid form of therapy by the British Medical Association in 1892–3. A report by a BMA sub-committee in 1955 also said that hypnotism has a part to play in medicine, and hundreds of doctors and dentists now use it as an additional form of treatment. Despite this, there is still considerable ignorance among the medical professions on the dynamics and uses of hypnotism, and the chances of an agoraphobe receiving such treatment are fairly arbitrary within the National Health Service. Unless an agoraphobe is fortunate enough to be treated by a member of the British Society for Medical and Dental Hypnosis, he will normally have to consult a lay hypnotist if he wants this form of treatment. As anyone can set themselves up as a hypnotist in Britain, whether well trained or not, due caution should be shown in selecting a therapist. (See 'Useful Addresses'.)

Hypnotism proved very useful in the treatment of my agoraphobia in two major areas. It speeded up the process of psychotherapy, accurately pinpointing the 'trouble spots' in my past life by bypassing the critical censor of my conscious mind. It could also produce a state of deep relaxation in me which I could not achieve in normal circumstances. Learning to relax through hypnosis helped to bring down my tension level and automatically lessened my vulnerability to panic attacks.

I had all the suspicions and fears of the uninformed about hypnosis: that I would not know what I was doing; that I might talk and reveal my secrets; that the therapist would be dominating my mind; and that I might not come out of hypnosis. My fears proved groundless, and I discovered that hypnosis is a state of relaxation which you allow yourself to enter, during which there is a state of altered conscious awareness.

Hypnotherapy brought dramatic improvement for a Yorkshire agoraphobe. A sufferer for 30 years, she found within five weeks of treatment that she could walk down the aisle at her son's wedding and was soon travelling by bus and car to local towns and taking walks around her own neighbourhood. Her son's wedding no doubt provided the necessary incentive for her to really get better, and hypnotism proved very effective in these circumstances.

In the hands of a trained professional, I found hypnosis to be a safe, sure and very pleasant form of therapy with no disadvantages or side-effects. It did not cure me, but it certainly helped a lot on the road to recovery. In the light of this, it is a great pity that British medical students are unlikely to receive a single lecture on hypnosis during their training. There are no special qualities attached to becoming a hypnotist, and the techniques can be learnt in the same way as any other therapy.

Hypnotism is a valuable adjunctive therapy in the treatment of agoraphobia and for the agoraphobe with purely emotional problems it can sometimes provide a cure. (See pp. 158–60.)

CARBON DIOXIDE (CO$_2$) THERAPY

As most agoraphobes and other anxiety sufferers tend to breathe from the apices of the lungs rather than utilising the whole of their breathing apparatus, the importance of deep natural breathing in combating anxiety symptoms has gained increasing recognition. Shallow breathing diminishes the supply of oxygen to the brain, contributing to feelings of dizziness, unreality or nausea.

Along with many other agoraphobes I am sure, I was totally unaware of my bad breathing habits since I had never breathed properly for years. Carbon dioxide (CO_2) rebreathing techniques forced my lungs to start working fully again until they did it spontaneously, resulting in a marked increase in anxiety tolerance and general calmness.

An agoraphobe wrote to me in great disgust about her doctor recommending her to blow into a paper bag in the street if she felt faint. However, as the main form of carbon dioxide therapy I used was breathing into a small plastic bag for a few moments until my lungs wanted to expand again, I cannot criticise this doctor's informed recommendation. It is obviously essential that the doctor explains the reasons behind carbon dioxide therapy to his patient, plus the fact that it can be done anywhere but preferably not in the open street where unnecessary self-consciousness would result, so raising the stress level instead of lowering it.

A pioneer in the field of carbon dioxide therapy is Arnold Orwin, who, as Consultant in Charge of the Regional Behaviour Research Unit, Hollymoor Clinic, Birmingham, has published the very positive results of respiratory relief (RR) and augmented respiratory relief (ARR) on phobic conditions (Orwin, 1971; 1973). Basic 'running treatment', where a phobia sufferer would be faced with the feared situation then sent to run round the block until completely breathless, could result in complete desensitisation particularly for specific phobias. A woman with a life-long fear of high-level water cisterns was given running treatment at Birmingham for five sessions, the cistern being raised higher each time. One month after the treatment ended the woman reported that she had completely lost her fear.

Carbon dioxide stimulates respiration and has a complex effect on the higher brain centres, which can result in the disappearance of stimulus-produced anxiety reactions. Arnold Orwin sought to intensify the therapy by giving the patient extra carbon dioxide in the form of a mixture of carbon dioxide and oxygen gas. By intensifying the patient's need to breathe he hoped to speed the effectiveness of desensitising treatment, a process which he called augmented respiratory relief. It worked, since therapy time was indeed lessened and the effects were more rapid than with ordinary respiratory relief, but the major disadvantage was that the treatment had to be medically supervised at all times. What Orwin has established is that if a patient is simultaneously exposed to the feared situation and given CO_2 therapy where he satisfies an intense desire to breathe, anxiety can be inhibited very effectively.

I used a form of running treatment quite inadvertently when, prior to any anxiety-provoking occasion, I would go for a stiff run across the fields to open my lungs and bring down my anxiety level. When I started doing this in the middle years of my agoraphobia I saw it as a practical way of expressing the 'fight or flight' instinct, releasing anxiety fears instantly in a very natural if slightly anticipatory way. This is a point which has been slightly missed by CO_2 therapists, but which I feel is central to the success of the treatment. In the same way, if I became breathless with fear in a sedentary situation such as driving my car, I would scream as hard as I could to release the pent-up anxiety and get my lungs working once more. Obviously I had to show some discretion when doing this since the sound can upset passers-by.

Orwin's major successes have been with specific phobias, but carbon dioxide therapy still has a definite place within the armoury of the agoraphobe. In its simpler forms it can be used by anyone, anywhere, and it can bring both short-term and long-term help to the agoraphobia sufferer, by stimulating proper breathing habits and releasing some of the anxiety.

Agoraphobes (or anyone else) should not attempt carbon dioxide therapy without first checking with their doctor or therapist. Once physical fitness has been established, the basic procedure should be outlined by the doctor so that any dangers to the patient can be eliminated.

HORMONE IMBALANCE

A theory which has been advanced by some doctors is that agoraphobia can be a direct result of hormone imbalance. In evidence they point out that many women have their first attack soon after having their first baby. Many women suffer most from panic attacks during the period of pre-menstrual tension, and some agoraphobia victims have been observed to be free of attacks while pregnant.

Hormone imbalance is now recognised as an important factor in the upsetting of women's normal mental and physical equanimity. In this sense it can precipitate agoraphobic tendencies by lowering stress tolerance levels, which are the critical factor where panic attacks are concerned. This is probably the only contribution hormone imbalance makes towards the onset and development of agoraphobia. It certainly goes no way towards explaining the cause of agoraphobia in men.

COMBINED THERAPIES

The chapter so far may have given the impression that each treatment is given separately to the agoraphobe, but it is far more common for combinations of therapies to be used.

For instance, psychologists at Rainhill Hospital, near Liverpool, used a form of behavioural therapy in combination with psychoanalytic techniques to help an agoraphobe who could not look at anything red. They traced her colour phobia back to the haemorrhages she suffered at the births of both her children. Over a period of four months they asked her to imagine that she was in a red room and to concentrate on meeting people wearing red clothes. By exposing her to her secondary phobia in this way, after a year of agoraphobia she could attempt to step beyond her front door.

Other treatments besides the major therapies listed here have been used, such as inducing anger in a patient to act as an anxiety inhibitor, and biofeedback machines which can help a patient to monitor and control his own stress level. All therapies generally have something to recommend them, and I recognise that suppressed aggression played a large part in the emotional side of my agoraphobia. Once I learnt I could lose my temper without losing my friends, my anxiety diminished and life became a lot easier. Anything which aids relaxation is good for agoraphobia, so biofeedback has its place for those who find it helpful.

The most usual combination of therapies in use at the present time is behavioural and drug therapy, and it is becoming increasingly clear that no single therapy will ever have the complete answer to agoraphobia. As no two agoraphobia sufferers are the same, so neither will ever respond in exactly the same way to whatever treatment is being administered. Constant awareness of the changing nature of agoraphobia should be maintained by the doctor so that available therapies can be utilised and modified to suit the individual's needs as he goes through the process of recovery.

Any complacency about the treatment currently medically available to agoraphobes should be very shortlived in the face of the cold facts of their rate of success. As 'consumers' for the various therapies, agoraphobes are well placed for accurate comment. Behaviour therapy has gained the highest praise from them, but even here less than one-third of those treated felt that it had been very helpful.

The therapies described here are not all available to every agoraphobe since a great deal depends on the part of the country in which they live. Perhaps this is the bitterest pill of all, since the agoraphobe by his very condition is often unable to get to other parts of the country where more sophisticated treatments may exist to help him. No wonder agoraphobes in general feel sadly neglected, and in most cases, rightly so.

It is clear from agoraphobes' accounts that there are still doctors and quite a few psychiatrists with little or no understanding of the condition, and with even less idea of how to treat agoraphobia if they do not recognise it.

vanish on its own after a few years, it is wrong for any doctor to
Although for a minority of sufferers agoraphobia can and does
assure patients that 'it often cures itself after several years.' For the
majority this does not happen, and they have to come to terms
with their huge disability as best they can. There cannot be an
agoraphobe, living or dead, who has not wished for the 'miracle
cure', where he can just sit back and wait for the wave of the magic
wand which will make everything all right again. It is unfair to
promise or suggest what is most unlikely, and further encourage
the agoraphobe to give up his heroic struggle for the sake of a
rather dubious 'pie in the sky'.

A woman from Northern Ireland summarised what is wanted
by most agoraphobia sufferers: 'My strongest feelings about what
is needed for agoraphobes is HELP. Constructive HELP. Not really
sympathy because no one can do it for you. Make the sufferer know
they can do it, should it take years. Family education, especially
for husbands who go out to work and do not really know what is
going on. A place where people can meet to talk, encourage, and
where everyone understands how everyone else feels. For those who
cannot go out, someone who could visit them and listen, talk and
get to know them, and be able to depend on them to come. Everyone who suffers from agoraphobia knows what it is like, but *it's
curing it that counts*.'

It would appear that no treatment method for agoraphobia has
yet been found by orthodox medicine which can consistently produce good results, let alone a cure. The most that can be claimed is
that the various therapies can help the agoraphobe to cope better
with his symptoms so he can lead a more normal existence, and
occasionally they can achieve a cure. Anyone who has been an
agoraphobe will know that this is scarcely enough, although it is a
lot better than no help at all.

REFERENCES

Beaumont, G. (1977). A Large Open Multicentre Trial of Clomipramine (Anafranil) in the Management of Phobic Disorders. *Journal of International Medical Research*, 5 (5), 116–123.

Editorial (1979). Treatments for Agoraphobia. *Lancet*, II, 8144, 679–680.

Marks, Isaac M. (1978). *Living with Fear. Understanding and Coping with Anxiety*, Chapter 12. McGraw-Hill Book Company, London and New York.

ibid, pp. 93; 202.

ibid, p. 199.

Mathews, A. Teasdale J., Munby M., Johnston D. and Shaw P. (1977). A Home-based Treatment Program for Agoraphobia. *Behavior Therapy*, 8 (5), 915–924.

Melville, J. (1977). *Phobias and Obsessions. Their Understanding and Treatment*, p. 35. George Allen and Unwin, London.

Orwin, A. (1971). Respiratory Relief: A New and Rapid Method for the Treatment of Phobic States. *British Journal of Psychiatry*, 119, 635–637.

Orwin, A. (1973). Augmented Respiratory Relief. A New Use for CO_2 Therapy in the Treatment of Phobic Conditions: A Preliminary Report on Two Cases. *British Journal of Psychiatry*, 122, 171–173.

Chapter 6

Treatment—The Alternative Approach

On the whole, agoraphobes do not like abandoning their own doctors and specialists when their treatments do not work, and they will put off the 'evil' day of seeing an alternative practitioner for as long as possible. However, when that day arrives as it does for so many, the agoraphobe will be in fairly desperate straits and he will have a tendency to clutch at any straw which is on offer. The alternative practitioner is also at a disadvantage since the agoraphobes who come to him are likely to be the most difficult cases. They arrive on his doorstep after all other therapies have failed and there is a tendency for them to want miracles which cannot be supplied.

Since alternative medicines are not subsidised by the National Health Service in Britain, the agoraphobe will have to pay for whichever treatment he selects. This may be the first time he has ever paid fully for medical treatment, which can be a psychological advantage since the incentive to make full use of the therapy he has bought will be so much stronger compared to his attitude to the 'free' treatment supplied by Government money. Even the psychological fact of personally selecting and going out to an alternative therapist indicates a certain faith and will to get better which may not have been there for orthodox methods.

The biggest surprise to the agoraphobe who goes for unorthodox treatment will probably be the amount of time the practitioner spends with him. Appointments will probably last between 30 minutes and one hour compared to the few moments the NHS doctor or specialist can usually afford, unless the patient has already been able to afford private treatment. The therapist can give each patient completely individual attention and will often tailor his therapy to fit individual needs, which may be an attitude the agoraphobe has not encountered previously.

As well as examining whether unorthodox medicine has anything new or valuable to offer the agoraphobe, this chapter will also be looking at orthodox alternatives which are available to the sufferer. Since some alternative treatments are accepted and practised by conventional doctors, the main criterion will be that the agoraphobe will generally have to seek private treatment from a medical or lay practitioner to obtain the therapy, or go to other outside agencies for the help he requires.

CLAIRE WEEKES' TREATMENT BY REMOTE DIRECTION

A consultant physician in Sydney, Australia, Claire Weekes is probably best known for her work in the study and treatment of agoraphobia. Her books, records, and radio and television appearances have ensured that her ideas have reached a wide international audience, including many a 'lost' agoraphobe. She describes her approach to treating anxiety states, especially the agoraphobic phase, as logical, simple and effective, and she claims considerable success for her methods. (See p. 184.)

Claire Weekes and her ideas are held in very high regard by phobic societies since she offers a self-help method which can be practised by all agoraphobes, and above all she gives the sufferer insight and understanding of the condition in a warm, clear style.

For instance, after three years of medical treatment a Welsh housewife who was still entirely unaware that she had agoraphobia happened to see Claire Weekes on television and greeted it as a revelation. She said: 'She was like the Archangel Gabriel! I got her book and read how I could actually *do* something when I got a panic attack. I read an explanation of the "jelly legs" and the detachment from reality which is so frightening when it happens ... But I'm attacking it. And I'm not mad. And I'm not even particularly selfish.'

Her experience is a typical one for many agoraphobes. To get over the problem of visiting agoraphobes in their own homes, Claire Weekes has developed her own system of treatment by remote direction. The agoraphobe can purchase books, long-playing records, cassettes and a quarterly magazine by the Australian doctor to help him on the spot, following her four basic principles of facing the fear, accepting the fear, floating past the fear and letting time pass. (See bibliography.)

By persuading the agoraphobe to face and work through the fear without fighting it, Claire Weekes aims to gradually desensitise the person so that fear eventually disappears. If the sufferer manages to follow her instructions faithfully this should happen, although complete cure is still rare. A drawback of her method is that it demands tremendous will-power on the part of the agoraphobe, and there is a danger that if the sufferer is unable to summon up the day-to-day motivation and courage to follow the instructions, or fails in the attempt, feelings of hopelessness and personal failure will be reinforced.

Even though cure does depend a great deal on the agoraphobe's will to get better, it is still very difficult to attempt to cure yourself on your own, even with the support of books and records. If agoraphobes do fail with self-help methods, they must not feel that it is the end of the line. The actual presence of a doctor or therapist may be necessary in their case to keep them going.

Claire Weekes' approach achieves the same end as most other therapies in that the agoraphobe's stress tolerance is gradually expanded so the likelihood of panic striking is correspondingly decreased. Her books and records are a boon for those who are frightened of seeking medical aid, or who are unlikely to receive any other specialist treatment.

PHOBIC SOCIETIES

'I thought it was never going to end. I wrote to Katherine Fisher of The Phobics Society as there was nobody else to ask. She wrote and told me to carry on and things would get better. That was nearly 12 months ago, and sure enough they did. I have been to London and I have been on holiday. I still have agoraphobia, but slowly I'm learning to cope with it, and the only person who taught me to cope is Katherine Fisher.'

These are the words of a state registered nurse who had already been through the hands of a doctor, a psychiatrist and a psychologist, and who found the only genuine help she received for agoraphobia was outside the National Health Service with a phobic society. Small wonder that such people as Mona Woodford, National Organiser of The Open Door Association, and Katherine Fisher, President of The Phobics Society, are hailed as 'guardian angels' by their many grateful members.

For a very small donation, the phobic societies and clubs provide a magnificent lifeline for their members, many of whom were completely bewildered and isolated before they joined. They are voluntary organisations run on a shoestring by a nucleus of dedicated workers. Any publicity on phobias in newspapers, on radio or television usually results in an avalanche of mail for them, but somehow the organisations manage to cope with the demand. Indeed there is a certain amount of rivalry between the various societies, which has a positive effect of better service to members.

Against their support and work for phobia sufferers one has to compare the rather miserable contribution from official Government and medical institutions. Agoraphobes still feel sadly neglected in many places, but the voluntary societies give them a straw to hang on to while they fight their own battle against their condition. Armed with the valuable knowledge that they are not on their own and that they are not going insane, the support of their societies helps them to see that there can be an end to their suffering. Practical help and information is on offer from the clubs in addition to their newsletters, such as the stocks of explanatory books and cassettes on phobias prepared by medical people from The Open Door Association, and The Phobics Society film—*Phobia —The Hidden Illness* which was awarded a Silver Certificate in the 1978 film competition run by the British Medical Association.

Similar organisations exist in the USA, where until a few years ago it was estimated that only one per cent of the nation's psychiatrists knew much about the treatment of agoraphobia, although the situation has since rapidly improved. A group of American sufferers founded Terrap (Territorial Apprehension) 18 years ago which runs a desensitisation programme for agoraphobes on lines laid down by Dr Arthur Hardy. His methods are used in 22 Terrap centres across the United States, which generally run a six months' programme with weekly lectures, a few also having two-week intensive programmes such as the Terrap centres in Menlo Park, California, and Memphis, Tennessee.

Although not related to Terrap, rather similar programmes are heavily based in the east of the USA. For instance, the Agoraphobia Treatment and Research Program at Temple University, Philadelphia, puts more stress on interpersonal problems as well as agoraphobia itself, and the University has compiled a general list of treatment facilities for agoraphobes.

The Phobia Clinic, White Plains Hospital, New York, was established in 1971 and is directed by Manuel D. Zane, who has developed a treatment called 'contextual analysis and therapy'. He treats the phobia in the actual setting in which the phobic reactions occur, helping the person to confront the situation in manageable steps. Rather like Claire Weekes he recommends patients to allow the fear to arise and accept it, and when it appears, to wait and try to remain focused on things in the present. The Phobia Clinic runs six eight-week clinics annually as well as running several self-help groups directed by 'phobia aides'—usually people who have had phobias and who have trained in contextual therapy under Dr Zane. Private individual and group sessions, outreach programmes, and a two-week course at White Plains or a correspondence course for out-of-town residents are also available.

A Phobia Society was organised at the Second Annual Phobia Conference held at Arlington, Virginia, in June 1980, with Manuel Zane and Arthur Hardy both being board members.

Small self-help groups calling themselves Agoraphobics Anonymous also exist in the USA. (See 'Useful Addresses'.)

ACUPUNCTURE

Acupuncture has been accepted as a valid therapy in the East for thousands of years. It is taught in several of Russia's universities, and with an estimated 5,000 practitioners in Europe it is gaining increasing acceptance in the West, with even more interest being shown in the USA.

Acupuncturists use needles of specially processed stainless steel which are used to gently pierce the skin at certain points along the Yin/Yang meridians—circuits rather like the blood, nerve and lymphatic circuits through which the body's life energy flows. Traditionally there are 800 of these points, although new ones continue to be found, and by piercing the skin the energy flow can be stimulated or sedated so that healthy equilibrium can be restored.

Such treatment is obtainable through national health schemes in many hospitals in France and Germany, and even in Britain orthodox medicine is showing definite interest in its possible use within the medical framework.

Whether or not one agrees with the theories behind acupuncture, its effectiveness in the treatment of such conditions as arthritis and rheumatism and its application as an anaesthetic are now fairly well substantiated. Rather less well known is its use in the treatment of depression and anxiety states and more rarely of agoraphobia. The Chairman of the British Acupuncture Association, Sidney Rose-Neil, said acupuncture could be used for agoraphobia and he has treated cases successfully, although no general statistics are available.

Julian Kenyon, a conventional doctor who is now specialising in acupuncture has treated quite a number of agoraphobia cases with 'really quite astonishing success'. Most of the sufferers responded to his treatment, and for those who carried the whole treatment through, the end results were very pleasing indeed.

Treatment for the agoraphobe consists of inserting five or six small needles into specific sites on the body, mainly the legs below the knees and the arms below the elbows (the forearm and the calf).

Contrary to expectation it does not hurt and can be quite pleasant, although some patients can find it a little uncomfortable.

An agoraphobic patient of the Liverpool doctor described her experience of acupuncture. She said: 'Agoraphobia started for me in 1971, although then I did not know what it was. I used to just freeze where I was, I couldn't move and I'd have the shakes. I was like this for two and a half years before my husband knew about it.' After unsuccessful drug treatment from her general practitioner and hospital specialist, she became housebound for a time but struggled on with a severely agoraphobic existence. 'I was in a sorry state when I went to Dr Kenyon but he is a very kind and understanding person. The doctor put three needles just above my toes, one either side of my ankles and three in my legs and three in each wrist. Since going to him [for 10 months] I can travel on my own in a taxi, walk a bit further by myself, go into supermarkets, go for a quiet drink with my husband and go out sometimes for a meal with him.'

She has also coped with looking after a sick parent and moving house, and in the meantime has needed less frequent appointments with fewer needles used during the treatment session. 'I say to anyone with agoraphobia, try acupuncture. Get help. Don't live a life of misery. I still have some shakes but they are not as bad and I can cope with them better,' she concluded.

Julian Kenyon gave his opinion on why acupuncture can help agoraphobia sufferers. He said: 'Basically it gets their "balance", as it were, right. Traditional Chinese medicine is the only system of medicine in the world which has a workable basis on which to particularise any patient's overall "balance". It really comes back to the basic idea of Yin/Yang which is just as relevant today as when it was first thought of some 4,000 years ago. Acupuncture and related forms of non-invasive medicine in my view go much more to treating the cause than allopathic [orthodox] medicine. I might add that in order to get the cause better you do not necessarily have to know what the cause is, and that is often the case of acupuncture and similar methods.'

In his experience there are very few doctors in Britain who

really understand traditional Chinese diagnosis, but as he and a few other doctors are teaching it to medical colleagues throughout the country he anticipates that acupuncture will eventually become available on the National Health Service.

Until that happy state of affairs is reached, agoraphobes will either have to seek private treatment from the few doctors specialising in acupuncture, or go to a lay practitioner. Lists of local medical practitioners are available from the British Medical Acupuncture Society and lists of lay acupuncturists who have reached their association's professional standards are available from the British Acupuncture Association, which is one of the many such associations formed throughout the world. In Britain there is nothing to prevent anyone trained or untrained setting up as an acupuncturist so due caution must be taken when considering this form of treatment. (See 'Useful Addresses'.)

OSTEOPATHY AND CHIROPRACTIC

Osteopathy concentrates on correcting spinal defects by manipulation, in the belief that people become ill if they are structurally unsound. Colin I. Dove of the General Council and Register of Osteopaths said that osteopaths do meet agoraphobia sufferers from time to time, but they are rarely consulted specifically for this problem. He has found that other symptoms often of a psychosomatic nature cause them to seek help, but on the whole the most an osteopath can do is offer a professional ear and advice tailored to the individual's needs, and attempt to remove the physical tension, which makes it possible for the patient to think more rationally and confidently.

It is possible to have osteopathic treatment from a doctor in the United Kingdom if he is a member of the British Osteopathic Association, and a number of doctors are members of the General Council and Register of Osteopaths which also includes lay practitioners who have reached a certain professional standard. The

British Naturopathic and Osteopathic Association also lists qualified lay practitioners.

In the USA there has been greater orthodox acceptance of osteopathy with many osteopaths being registered as doctors of medicine rathers than doctors of osteopathy.

Chiropractic also uses various manipulative techniques and is an accepted and popular therapy in many parts of the world, particularly the USA, Canada, and Switzerland. In Britain there are less chiropractors per head of population than in 10 other major countries, with the British Chiropractors' Association being confined mainly to the south of England.

A. C. Breen, Research Officer of the British Chiropractors' Association said that chiropractors seldom treat agoraphobia as an exclusive complaint although they do see it quite frequently in versions of other complaints concerning mechanical disorders of the spine. Statistics of presentation are very low so he did not think he could offer a chiropractic solution to agoraphobia.

HOMOEOPATHY

Homoeopathy is a medical system where the doctor will treat the patient with minute doses of drugs which will produce similar symptoms to the illness from which he is suffering, believing that 'like should be treated by like'. Homoeopathy is accepted by the British health authorities and theoretically it is available on the National Health Service although the numbers of doctors who have done extra training in homoeopathy have diminished over the years.

Maureen Munday, General Secretary of The British Homoeopathic Association, said that agoraphobia has been known to respond to homoeopathic treatment and that homoeopathy is of considerable value in the management of such disorders. Due to the very general nature of the homoeopathic physician's approach to the treatment of any cases, unfortunately no details, statistics or case histories are available on agoraphobia.

YOGA

Yoga is usually seen as a means of keeping fit and of becoming more relaxed in mind and body, but its application can go much deeper than this, giving genuine help to the agoraphobe.

Howard Kent, Director of the Yoga for Health Foundation, a registered charity, said that yoga is especially useful in dealing with agoraphobia and that he knew of a number of cases where it has totally removed the problem. He said: 'The most important thing is to understand the part which breathing plays in our lives. The form of society we have created both from the physiological and the mental stress point of view depletes—and in many cases virtually destroys—our natural breathing patterns. The breath always mirrors our state of mind and body, and when we are tense or worried the breath becomes irregular and panting; control of the out-breath virtually disappears. This is because the out-breath is the relaxation and letting-go part of our system.

'The respiratory process is an amazing one because, while basically autonomic [not directly under conscious control], it permits the greatest possible degree of voluntary control. Through exercising this control we can create an internal situation which gives us the foundation upon which major changes can be created. Thus the agoraphobic terror can be arrested through control of the breath and this then provides a stepping stone towards the creation of a more "normal" life pattern.

'At the same time we need to move away from the tyranny of so-called thoughts which are almost all a sequence of memories. Yoga helps us to develop awareness, so that inhibiting-thought becomes less and less active. In agoraphobia, for example, the predominant thought is, "I can't do it ...", "I'm afraid ...", "I remember how afraid it makes me ..." etc. To counter this by a more positive thought demands that first of all we diminish the bad thought itself, and this is achieved by performing quite simple movements with awareness and related to the flow of the breath.

'Persistent application is very important but these things cannot be forced—the wrong set of determination is itself a stress application and can be counter-productive. Linking the breath with body posture in awareness helps to create this right basis. The vital thing is to begin to create a calmness of mind, and basic yoga postures, correctly performed, will help to achieve this.'

Yoga with its emphasis on relaxation, breathing and posture will bring positive help to the agoraphobia sufferer, who normally is affected by tense, shallow breathing and limited physical movement. As the Yoga for Health Foundation puts it: 'All too often our minds are like a tree full of chattering birds, flying, apparently aimlessly, from branch to branch. Yoga postures enable us to quiet the chattering and limit the aimless flight.' However, its use to a largely housebound population is severely limited, since professional tuition in yoga would appear to be essential for good results.

DIET, HERBS AND NATURE

Diet can play an important part in helping agoraphobia sufferers to keep fit and healthy, and there is also a possibility that food allergies may be aggravating or even, according to some authorities, causing the agoraphobia.

Richard Mackarness's book *Not All in the Mind* (Pan Books, 1980 edition) has given a fascinating view on how unsuspected food allergy can affect the body and mind, and Julian Kenyon has found that some of his agoraphobic patients have food sensitivities which can help resolve their problems. Using his own techniques for locating these, he has found that he 'can usually sort them out by sorting their diet out'.

Although conventional medicine does not officially recognise herbalism the 1968 Medicines Act gave herbalists legal recognition as consultants, and tens of thousands of people in England are presently seeking regular treatment. A Midlands herbalist practice with four consultants has well in excess of 60,000 people on its books who come for the 'whole body' and 'whole mind' approach which has belonged to herbalists from Hippocrates' time and before.

As well as recommending a natural wholefood diet, herbalists use the whole plant of any herb in their preparations, believing it contains its own natural buffers against side-effects. John D. Hyde, President of Britain's National Institute of Medical Herbalists, also emphasises the dietary aspects of phobia, giving the simple analogy of how oats, which are rich in vitamin B and sativine, can cause horses to be over-reactive. There are a whole range of herbal remedies prescribed individually for phobia sufferers, including piscidia, pulsatilla, scutellaria, cypripedium and panax quinque-folium.

Naturopaths equally stress the importance of diet in the treatment of phobias. For complete health, diet must be of foods for which man is adapted, which does not include refined, artificially preserved or concentrated food. Instead one should eat unspoiled produce such as fruits, vegetables, cereals, nuts and dairy produce. Naturopathy looks at man as a unity of mind, body and ethos, believing the basic cause of illness is an imbalance between these planes. According to naturopaths, no drugs are necessary in the treatment of illness since we give ourselves our illnesses, and they place a lot of emphasis on the elimination of toxic matter within the body through fasting, diet and hydrotherapy (water treatment) in order to regain a proper balance.

Michael A. van Straten of the British Naturopathic and Osteopathic Association said that association members have achieved considerable success in the treatment of agoraphobia disorders. By a combination of psychological knowledge and by introducing patients to sound nutrition, remarkable improvements had been achieved in many psychosomatic disorders, including many of the common phobias.

From my own experience I would recommend all agoraphobes to try a wholefood diet—as long as it is not going to cause more stress than it is worth in trying to get hold of the 'right' foods. I began trying out a natural diet after interviewing a herbalist for a newspaper feature and the contribution it has made to my general well-being stood me in very good stead while working through the physical ravages of my final years of agoraphobia. I never realised what an awful effect such foods as cream, white flour, red meat, tea and coffee could have on me when taken in excess until I had stopped eating them for a while. The only rules I adhere to are: avoid all food which has been refined or which contains preservatives or additives of any sort, and, don't be a bore about it once you do get 'hooked' on to natural wholefoods—the occasional 'relapse' does no particular harm.

OTHER THERAPIES

There are now hundreds of therapies available outside conventional medicine coming under the general headings of physical therapies, hydrotherapy, nutrition, plant-based therapies, radiation and vibration, mind and spirit therapies and self-exercise. Agoraphobes have almost certainly tried them all in their efforts to find a cure, but it would be impossible to run a survey on their effectiveness without expanding this book to twice its present size.

As all agoraphobes are individuals there is probably something of value for a certain type of sufferer in nearly every treatment, and I am not the person to dismiss anything which may be of help to sufferers from this gigantic problem.

Physical therapies such as deep soft tissue manipulation, Rolfing, dance, gymnastic and sport therapies can be used to release physical tensions and to concentrate the mind on the inner peace which can be reached through physical activity. Emmett W. Hutchins of the Rolf Institute in Boulder, Colorado, said that Rolfers are confident that Rolfing does work to release the expression of fear at any level, although no specific data was available on the treatment of agoraphobia. Rolfing is a method developed in the USA by Ida Rolf which involves deep soft tissue techniques which release postural, mechanical and psychic tensions. A consistent result of their methods is claimed to be a decrease in social introversion and a shift towards a more open, outgoing, extroverted personality.

The Alexander technique developed by F. Matthias Alexander has been in use for over 80 years in the USA, the United Kingdom and other countries. Its teachers claim that bad posture and muscular tension can be the cause of many common complaints such as backaches, arthritis and mental stress. It is difficult to learn since it is a process of re-education of everything involving muscles, and at least 30 individual lessons are needed to get useful results. Wilfred Barlow, who wrote *The Alexander Principle* (Arrow Books, 1979 edition), believes that once the initial difficulty of getting the agoraphobia sufferer to come to the consulting rooms for treatment has been overcome, the Alexander technique can be very valuable. As phobic states are usually associated with both generalised and localised muscular hypertension, he claims that a deconditioning method such as the Alexander technique is acceptable to the patient and rewarding in its results.

Self-help techniques of any sort are bound to be more attractive to the agoraphobe who has such difficulties in getting out for any sort of treatment. Co-counselling is a method of mutual self-help which avoids seeking the help of an 'expert'. Anne Dickson of the London Co-counselling Community explained that co-counselling promotes the belief that we can reach an understanding of our own feelings and their sources on our own, and with supportive attention we can distinguish patterns in our behaviour which prevent us from achieving what we want. Participants learn a variety of simple techniques which enable them to reach areas of stored distress and to release it physically. As the hurt is released, so they gain insight into what has happened to them, so freeing themselves from the restrictive effect of their early negative conditioning. Anne Dickson believes that by learning to discharge his fear, an agoraphobic person could learn to manage his particular feared situations.

Every anxiety state including agoraphobia produces bodily changes including an increased heart rate and a galvanic skin response (GSR). Microscopic levels of perspiration at the finger-tips can be measured and monitored by biofeedback instruments which can help agoraphobes to assess their anxiety level and to gradually desensitise themselves. Biofeedback can be used privately (if you can afford the instruments), helping the sufferer to mechanically monitor the body processes by visual display and audible signal. The biofeedback principle is: 'If you can become aware of some body pattern of which you are not normally aware, then you can control that function.' Biofeedback instruments indicate by electronically activated devices the states of mind and body of the person using them, so that involuntary manifestations of stress can be measured and gradually controlled. An agoraphobe could learn to bring down his stress level in this way, so decreasing the chances of panic.

Overall stress levels can also be reduced by learning progressive relaxation, where a deep level of relaxation can be achieved by muscle relaxation and the suspension of anxious thoughts. Transcendental meditation techniques are also useful for reducing inner stress and turmoil.

SPIRITUAL HEALING

Prayer is undoubtedly of great help to those agoraphobes with strong religious convictions, bringing them some aid and peace among their tribulations. In their constant search for a cure, some agoraphobes have sought a 'miracle' in the true sense, looking to God to bring them recovery when all else has failed. Although faith healing and spiritual or divine healing would appear to be the same thing, with the healer laying his hands on the afflicted person and praying for his recovery, there is a distinct difference at least in theory. Spiritual healers see themselves totally as instruments of God, with any healing power deriving directly from Him rather than having any specific 'power' themselves.

Whatever the theoretical background, it would appear that certain people do have a healing quality which has brought peace to some agoraphobes. A 43-year-old Selkirkshire mother who had had agoraphobia for most of her adult life described how spiritual healing eventually helped her to overcome the majority of her symptoms. She said: 'Four years ago I was housebound, having been in that state for two years. The rest of my life consisted of spells of relative freedom to go shopping at the nearest corner shop and to travel short distances in the family car. This was an all-time low and nothing seemed to help. I had tried all the self-help methods available and I knew more about agoraphobia than the psychiatrist did! But I could not go over the doorstep.'

In 1976 a friend told her of a Baptist minister who 'had been greatly used by God in the healing ministry'. She arranged for a visit from the minister who laid his hands on her and prayed for her recovery.

'After his visit I suffered three of the most terrible days I had had for a long time, but I had been given a book by someone about praising God in all things, so even through my tears of depression, I kept repeating: "Thank you Lord for healing me." On that third day, my husband asked me if I would like to go out in the car. I had not been out for two years.

'I went 27 miles in the car that day and was like a prisoner who had just been let out. I jumped up and down like a child. "Look at the trees, oh aren't they beautiful?" (It was autumn and the glory of the colours really hit me.) Going through our town I felt like Rip Van Winkle must have done after his long sleep. Everything seemed to have changed, new shops had sprung up like mushrooms, new housing estates.

'We stopped outside a shop to buy some cakes. I was afraid to go as I hadn't been inside a shop for over two years and my memories of panicking in shops were very much alive. However, something seemed to be prompting me: "Get out of the car." Slowly I opened my door and gingerly eased my shaking legs out on to the unfamiliar hardness of the pavement. I stood, one hand on the door handle, then I let go and looked at the street. It seemed so unreal to be standing there. Then suddenly I was in the queue with my mother and son, waiting to buy the cakes. Never did any cake taste so good!'

She then got a job as caretaker at the Baptist church, and although she could not do everything, 'very gradual' improvement took place until she hit a set-back of very bad depression which she had not had before during her agoraphobia. She rang her minister friend to tell him she was as bad as ever, and he recommended her to contact the Christian Fellowship of Healing (Scotland) in Edinburgh.

She said: 'I haven't looked back since I first contacted the Fellowship. There I was able to find out what things were hindering the completion of my wholeness. Childhood memories, festering resentments, suppression by my parents of my natural creativity, over-emphasis on the "thou shalt nots". I was able, with the minister's help, to let Jesus go back with me into the past, relive the experiences which had caused me to become an anxious fearridden creature, and let him heal those scars.

'That was in October 1978. In September 1979 I purchased my moped. Now I go all over town on my own and my greatest joy is to bike up to the highest hill in town and look down on the houses in the valley far below. It is the biggest, widest open space imaginable. I can see the Cheviot Hills, the range separating Scotland and England. I can also see a vision of a road, the road of life stretching out before me, widening out in the most exciting way. I feel reborn.'

She admitted that she still had problems, finding it difficult to walk outside or sit in a church, concert hall or anywhere where there were crowds of people. She said: 'I have no doubts that just as the Lord has wiped so many of my fears away, he will deal with the remaining ones in his time, not mine. I can wait, knowing that "he is faithful and he will do it." '

A 38-year-old Sheffield mother who had been severely agoraphobic attributed her recovery to spiritual or divine healing. In 1977 after the death of her youngest sister she suddenly decided to attend a church service. She said: 'I accepted Jesus that night and the pastor prayed for me. I still suffered from agoraphobia, but that is when the Lord began healing. I stopped my diazepam [Valium] tablets and had terrible withdrawals. I began to take a smaller dosage tablet. I then had an inner desire to go out.

'I began taking my washing outside without holding the wall.

I prayed each time I ventured out. I found out that each time I took a step with God's help I was great, but each time I was out without consulting Him I had my old fears.'

She said it had been a 'gradual healing', but now she could attend such things as meetings at the city hall and a Sunday school Whit walk without any help from drugs or other therapies.

A 40-year-old Banbury housewife told a dramatic story of recovery which she attributed wholly to the power of Christ. After a 'nervous breakdown' while doing her O-levels at school, she began to suffer from feelings of unreality and she was unable to face any social events or attend any crowded function by the time she went to university. As a student in London, she feared going out on the Underground or walking along a street with other people, particularly a long, unbroken street with no 'bolt holes'. She struggled through two years of university, and in her final year her doctor decided that she needed psychiatric help, but this failed to cure her.

She said: 'One day I was moved to attend a Quiet Day arranged by the Anglican Chaplaincy at the University Church. During the day there was the opportunity to make one's confession. Totally unprepared and very confused, I made an extremely brief and halting statement of my fears and depression to the confessor. With the absolution, a great sense of joy and certainty came flooding into my being and from that moment on, most of my self-doubt and depression melted away.

'For a time I felt as though I was walking on air and I think my psychiatrist wondered what had happened to me when I went for my next—and final—counselling session. Since that time I have not looked back and am happily married to a schoolmaster and have three children and a teaching job. Although my cure did not take place in a specific context of divine healing, I attribute it wholly to the power of Christ.'

In the 1977 National Survey of Agoraphobics almost exactly the same number of agoraphobes who had been to see a religious or spiritual healer said they had found it very helpful. (See p. 183.)

It is worth observing that a religious minister or confessor and a psychologist, psychiatrist, psychotherapist or even an ordinary doctor fulfil rather similar roles for the agoraphobe. They all, theoretically, lend a ready ear to the agoraphobe's story and offer help and guidance in unravelling the possible causes of the agoraphobia and helping the sufferer to come to terms with them.

Faith in God can also reinforce the agoraphobe's will to live and ultimate belief that he can indeed get better. It is also a great help to believe that you are not alone in your agoraphobic struggle and that supernatural help outside yourself is available to help you through the Herculean task of getting better.

It has been estimated that over one million people in Britain now consult alternative practitioners, which shows an appreciable dissatisfaction with the results of conventional medicine. Undoubtedly, some agoraphobes have found the answers to their problems through alternative treatments, and their successes are very welcome in a situation where so many agoraphobes are finding little or no relief.

The general antipathy of the orthodox medical world towards alternative therapies may be more professional than real, since such treatments as osteopathy, acupuncture, hypnotism and homoeopathy are already practised by some conventional doctors as well as their lay counterparts.

The biggest danger in Britain is that there is no legalisation to prevent anyone setting themselves up as an 'instant' hypnotist or acupuncturist which is neither fair to the ethical therapist nor to a highly vulnerable and sometimes desperate section of the community. Trying to wipe out the various therapies in the simple belief that only conventional treatments are 'right' for people would be an insupportably doctrinaire attitude and not one supported by facts, nor is there much logic in believing that only orthodox doctors are capable of handling the multitude of therapies available outside hospital walls. A government's energies would be more sensibly directed towards a constructive assessment of practitioners' abilities and training schemes outside orthodox circles, with a system of licensing which would protect both the ethical practitioner and the general public.

As far as agoraphobes are concerned, alternative treatments can give new hope and incentives to get better, they can often help sufferers to cope better with their symptoms and occasionally they can achieve cure. As in orthodox treatments, none could claim to have achieved the elusive goal of consistent cure for agoraphobia. The answer, again, would appear to lie elsewhere.

Chapter 7

The New Approach

The Institute for Neuro-Physiological Psychology is presently situated in Stanley Place, Chester, but its considerable achievements and research are probably better known and appreciated in Sweden and the USA than in the British Isles. Heading the team is Director of the Institute, psychologist Peter Blythe, who has spent a good deal of his life trying to understand the dynamics underlying both mental and physical disorders. He and his co-Director David McGlown, who together founded the Institute, have presented their findings on an organic (physical) basis for neuroses (mental illness) in several papers, together with their major work of pinpointing why children who are not 'backward' or emotionally disadvantaged can continually fail at school. These and their book *An Organic Basis for Neuroses and Educational Difficulties* (Insight Publications, Chester, 1979) have aroused much interest abroad, with Sweden recently establishing its own sister Institute in Gothenburg.

In contrast to normal medical experience, there are no white coats or formal attitudes at the Chester Institute. Patients sit in comfortable chairs and the therapists listen carefully to everything which they have to say, with none of the 'us' and 'them' attitudes frequently found in other often less successful medical circles.

When Peter accepted me for treatment at the end of 1973 I had no idea of the research programme which was underway or what a huge turning-point it was to provide in my treatment. I feel the best introduction to this new concept in therapy is the subjective evidence of my own first-hand experience, with a more general explanation being given in the next chapter.

After two and a half years of intensive psychoanalysis and

hypnotherapy I was improved beyond all hope, but my progress was still painfully slow and I could only function in very limited areas. Because I was not making the progress he would have hoped for within the therapy, it was at this point that Peter asked me if I would undergo a series of tests which the Institute was using on children with learning problems, just to see if there were any physical, neurological or emotional impediments to my recovery as yet undetected. The application of these tests to adults was very much in its infancy, but I was happy to try anything which might help.

David McGlown conducted the five and a half hours' examination, and it took a further eight working hours for the results of the tests to be put together. In line with the Institute's policy of keeping patients fully informed, I, as well as my therapist, received a copy of the results.

The 14-page document made fascinating reading. Not only had the personality tests revealed my character precisely and most uncomfortably (David had never met me before the tests), but there was also neurological evidence of minimal or organic brain dysfunction—difficulties of functioning caused by small faults within the central nervous system. My gross muscle coordination was not very good, and I had such problems with eye muscle movement that to focus my eyes on an object cost me a great deal more effort than for people with normal eyes.

The mention of brain dysfunction, albeit minimal, sounds far more frightening than it really is. Most people have a little brain dysfunction, perhaps resulting from a difficult delivery, the use of forceps, a feverish illness such as scarlet fever, pneumonia or whooping cough, or other environmental factors. The question is not really whether you have brain dysfunction, but to what extent you have it, and whether it interferes with your day-to-day living. The brain can and does compensate, but sometimes the compensation can be a little too much for a person to cope with.

There is nothing particularly new in detecting signs of minimal brain dysfunction (MBD), or organic brain dysfunction (OBD) as it has been more strictly defined by Peter Blythe and David

McGlown since 1972. The name was changed by them since minimal brain dysfunction has never been strictly defined and means different things to different people. 'Minimal' also implies 'a little', but recent research has shown that even a tiny amount of brain dysfunction can cause huge problems. The Institute's major contribution in this field is that besides detecting organic brain dysfunction, it can measure how much dysfunction a person has and can remedy it—something which has never been done before in medical history.

It is important to remember that my OBD treatment, which lasted three years, only went as fast as the research programme was progressing, and the more significant findings were only made towards the end of the 10 years' research period in 1979. Hence the detection of more primitive dysfunctions came last for me, whereas clients today can expect to have all their dysfunctions or otherwise detected at the same time, with a complete treatment programme given from the start.

For myself, the treatment devised by the Institute took the form of 20 minutes' physical and eye exercises which were to be done once a day at home. In addition I had to wear an eye-patch over my non-dominant left eye whenever I could but not on social occasions, and I had to breathe into a plastic bag every hour for one minute to improve the use of my lungs. (See p. 110.) The main drawback of the exercise programme was that it could get very boring once the initial excitement had died down, and it also took a lot of will power of a different kind to wear the eye-patch in a newspaper office, where I was tormented for weeks with jokes about parrots and pirates. Although the Institute did not insist on this I chose to do it to speed up my recovery.

The effect of this first exercise programme was immediate. I had unconsciously been using my left eye for sighting when doing close work, but on the first day of wearing the eye-patch, which took the stress off my eye muscles and forced me to focus with my right eye, my temper improved dramatically. Within a short time I found I could work for longer periods without getting tired and the feelings of unreality and depersonalisation slowly diminished.

As time went on I found I could run properly for the first time in my life with all my muscles working together, and even my tennis took an unexplained and sudden turn for the better. Uncharacteristically, I stopped worrying about losing and just enjoyed the game for itself.

I went back every three months for reassessment, which took approximately two hours of David's time. My progress was checked and as the research progressed, new tests were made and the exercise programme modified as necessary. The two most significant discoveries as far as I was concerned were the detection of the presence of a spinal (Galant) primitive reflex on the right hand side of my spine plus a defective labyrinthine righting reflex, both of which should have been inhibited and modified in early infancy. (See p. 155.) Up to this point no one had suspected that these reflexes could still exist in normal adults so the testing itself was an entirely new departure by the Institute.

The spinal (Galant) reflex was named after its discoverer in 1917, and as it is possible to obtain it in a fetus of 20 weeks it is considered to be very ancient, in evolutionary terms. It is a pure skin reflex where the back is stroked near and along the vertebral column causing the body to arch in the direction of the stimulus. The reflex should disappear in early infancy but if it persists beyond six months it can interfere with the achievement of sitting balance. That I still responded to it on the right hand side of my spine when I was 35 years old came as a complete surprise to everyone.

The permanent correction of the spinal (Galant) reflex took only 15 minutes—five minutes' exercise on three consecutive days—and again the effect was quite dramatic. I had never been able to get rid of the permanent tension around my lower abdomen, but suddenly it disappeared. The lower part of my body felt in harmony for the first time in my life and tension build-up in that area became very rare indeed. This further resulted in the relaxation of my lower digestive system, and my colon ceased to give me diarrhoea except when under extreme stress or weariness, which happened far less frequently.

It was found that my agoraphobic tendencies of feeling dizzy, seasick and sometimes 'unreal' were very much tied up with the labyrinthine canals of the inner ear which were not functioning efficiently enough for me to be always aware of my proper place in space.

The balancing structures within the inner ears, together with our eyes, inform our brains exactly where we are in space, and they are particularly sensitive to motion. This is one reason why people who are seasick tend to feel better if they keep their heads still and their eyes closed. It is also the reason why people who are prone to motion sickness find it easier to travel after dark, since they cannot see where they are in space and the brain is less confused. Fresh air also acts as an antidote to travel sickness which is no doubt why I, like many other agoraphobes, prefer to travel with car windows open. The importance of the eyes and balancing structures are reflected quite unconsciously by agoraphobes themselves. The majority mention dizziness, nausea, feeling unreal and being afraid of falling over.

Today's research is laid on old foundations, for even Hippocrates' description nearly two and a half thousand years ago says the sufferer 'loves darkness as life and cannot endure the light or to sit in lightsome places; his hat still in his eyes, he will neither see, nor be seen by his good will . . .' It is also recognised that dark glasses often afford relief to agoraphobia sufferers.

As early as 1770, F. B. de Sauvages wrote of the giddiness of phobia sufferers in general, calling the condition *vertigo hysterique*, since he thought vertigo was the major factor of the disorder (Sauvages, 1770–1). One hundred years later, M. Benedikt regarded giddiness as the hallmark of agoraphobia, calling the disorder *Platzschwindel*, meaning literally a public place where you get giddy. He was already ascribing the dizziness to dysfunction of the eye muscles (Benedikt, 1870).

Many of the typical clinical features for the onset of agoraphobia seem to reflect the malfunctioning of the balancing reflex—lightness and dizziness in the head, suddenly feeling ill, weakness of the legs, having an illusion of walking on shifting ground, and

fear of fainting or collapsing. A test for Romberg's sign (which in-
cidentally was a test used by police for suspected drunkenness) will
often result in an agoraphobe swaying or even falling over. The
agoraphobe will have been asked to stand erect with the eyes closed
and the feet placed together. If the balancing mechanisms are in
working order, there should be little perceptible sway, since the
person has not lost his place in space even with the eyes shut.

To try and rectify the balancing disorder, the Institute followed
its usual procedure of giving its patients a 'second chance' to go
back through the stages of motor (bodily movement) development
which they should have gone through as a child. Somehow I had
to be removed from my adult environment and be put into a new
one where the reflex which was missing could be stimulated and
built up.

When the USA's National Aeronautics and Space Administration started its moon programme, there were to be many practical spin-offs for modern man from sending astronauts into space,
non-stick pans being one most housewives will recognise. To help
acclimatise astronauts to space conditions, NASA introduced spinning and 'bouncing' techniques which took away all normal sensations of gravity and position in space.

Taking a leaf from the American's book, the Institute developed
another exercise programme, based on these techniques, in an attempt to develop the reflexes of my inner ear. If they worked for
astronauts in space, the chances were they would work for me.
Following Peter's specifications, Jim built several large pieces of
equipment which would rotate or spin a human body in a variety
of positions: prone, supine, sitting, moving up and down—so that
complete vestibular stimulation of the semicircular canals in the
inner ear became possible.

The first time I was spun round on one of the pieces of equipment, within minutes I got all my agoraphobic symptoms: dizziness, nausea and the desire to vomit and defaecate. Gradually I
managed to take longer periods of the exercises, and the tension
round my eyes, jaws, neck and shoulders correspondingly lessened

and my eyes worked more efficiently for longer periods and with less strain.

The most exciting result from these vestibular exercises came when Jim had put together the last piece of equipment and invited me to get on it to test it for size and efficiency. He rotated me horizontally to the left only, and for three days afterwards I developed an alarming tendency to overbalance quite helplessly, with head spinning, but always on the left hand side. I did not connect the events until we began the exercises properly three days later, and when I was rotated to the right I got a similar spinning sensation on the right hand side of my head—almost as if marbles were rattling into place in my head. It only happened once on each side of my head and the rectification was complete.

Just as the correction of the spinal (Galant) reflex had brought peace to the lower part of my body, the correction of this vestibular righting reflex had a similarly profound effect on the upper part of my body. Always a bad sleeper, I suddenly began to sleep very deeply and for much longer than normal. My natural aggressiveness began to manifest itself very clearly and my temperament became markedly more even. Uncharacteristically and quite spontaneously I began to take life as it came and to make 'spur of the moment' decisions, and a natural joie de vivre began to appear.

Visually I was already much improved, but a further improvement was apparent. Going for a run across the fields I was immediately conscious that I was aware of the full visual field, not just a small area immediately ahead, which was all I normally saw while running, and the running itself was more pleasant with a serenity of vision I had not had before. My photosensitivity lessened markedly, and my eyes were consistently bright and shining even after a full day's close study of reading material, where once my eyes would have been bloodshot and dim. Recovery rate from both mental and physical exertion became very rapid where once it would take me days if not weeks to revitalise myself.

Besides my defective labyrinthine righting reflex it was also found that I had no segmental rolling reflex and no parachute reflex, which in simple layman's terms meant that I had no natural instinct or reflex to protect myself if I did fall over. From early childhood I had an acute fear of falling over which would stop me from doing anything remotely 'dangerous', such as jumping across a ditch, jumping off a moving bus as it approached a stop, climbing or jumping from any height, or even running. My physical movement was very restricted even before I had agoraphobia through this fear of falling over, which was out of all proportion to the damage I might incur. I instinctively knew I could not cope with such movements so I kept well away from any vigorous physical activity. Unconsciously I was protecting myself from very real defects in development which happened during my infancy.

Quite logically, the exercises I was given to combat this deficiency forced me to protect myself spontaneously, until my 'saving' reactions were properly established. My unnatural fears of falling were at an end, giving me increased confidence and freedom of movement.

Throughout the exercise programme, I received psychotherapeutic support since occasionally the exercises can trigger off all sorts of traumas from the past, almost as if the 'going back in time' in motor development is paralleled in the emotions. This does not happen for the majority of patients, but what I did find was that the psychotherapeutic side of my treatment was greatly accelerated as a result of the success of the exercises. (See p. 164.) I galloped through a series of emotional explosions which I would not have been able to tolerate previously, so clearing away the remains of my 'secondary' neuroses. I now knew my emotional problems were not primary at all, but had appeared largely as a result of my organic brain dysfunctions.

As I worked my way through the residue of my emotional problems and anxiety, the correction of my various dysfunctions revealed itself in many other ways. Once my labyrinthine righting reflex had been corrected, the depersonalisation or derealisation which I suffered during my more schizoid moments as an agoraphobe disappeared without trace. Prior to this I should most certainly have retreated into depersonalisation with the stress of the accelerated emotional conflicts I was undergoing, but I was physiologically unable to do so. Somehow I had been pushed into reality for good with no facility for retreating into unreality as I had in the past.

This meant I was very much more exposed to my emotional problems because I could not get away from them, and therapeutic cure began to resemble more of a 'short sharp shock' than the gentler progress I had managed to maintain before. It was very painful but in a rather different way since my being was now equipped to take the reality to which it was consistently being exposed. With my body in natural harmony I hurtled willy-nilly down the final stretch of the road to recovery.

The practical result of this treatment was that within the space of 12 months I progressed from making a difficult and panicky car journey to Chester to flying on holiday in Switzerland with comparative ease. As I have said before, it is not how far you get that counts in terms of getting better from agoraphobia, but how you actually do it. Within six weeks of the correction of my labyrinthine righting reflexes I went on a skiing, skating and tobogganing holiday, which was something I would not have contemplated even prior to agoraphobia, with my fear of falling down; and within the next three months I flew to America to attend the opening of a new museum and to research a new book.

On a professional scale, from being able to work intensively for two hours then having to take the rest of the day off to recover, I could work for a full day and be relaxed and able to 'switch off' at the end of it. I left my newspaper employment and became a successful freelance writer and publicity consultant.

In the space of a year, from being too terrified to face a group of people, I tutored a Workers' Educational Association summer course, an adult studies course in a college of higher education, gave visiting lectures to university graduate and postgraduate courses, and gave a paper to an international history congress. I also gave talks to a diversity of groups ranging from the local Civic Trust to a Conservative Ladies Luncheon Club in order to flex my unused speaking muscles and lay the bogey of my agoraphobia. I had been a successful lecturer before my agoraphobia, but after my

OBD programme I found that I could lecture without notes—something I would never have dared to do before. I presented two radio series and found that under the greatest pressure I would always remember what I was talking about even without a script. More importantly I began to enjoy myself instead of viewing life as an endless series of hurdles over which I was required to jump until I finally dropped dead with exhaustion.

On the domestic side I began to run a home and be a farmer's wife without thinking about it, and socially I enjoyed whatever came my way. From being utterly terrorised by visitors, they were welcome once more in my home and Flint, my Rhodesian ridgeback, trotted back into the house to take up happy round-the-clock residence with us.

There is a danger that by lumping together all the professional and personal signs of my recovery in a few paragraphs, I may have given a misleading impression that my progress was easy and that I had indeed found a 'miracle' cure. In one sense the OBD programme did create a 'miracle' in that it laid straight the paths for my complete recovery, which otherwise would have been quite impossible to achieve. On the other hand, the total and unremitting effort to get out and conquer the physical or behavioural manifestations of agoraphobia still had to be made every day, until the symptoms began to vanish for good and the fear of the fear was finally laid to rest. As already described there was also a residue of emotional problems to be worked through and resolved before I had complete peace of mind.

But the major difference after the exercise programme was that the remaining physical and emotional difficulties were conquered infinitely more rapidly as a result of the Institute's work, because all impediments to successful therapy had been removed. As I progressed, I found that my problems began to take on a different aspect becoming increasingly more reality-based.

I vividly recall the time when I took the plunge and accepted my first speaking engagement for many years. Apprehensively anticipating my agoraphobic symptoms in such a stressful situation, I spent a nervous fortnight preparing the talk and was predictably very ill indeed in the two hours before I went in front of my audience. I fully expected to panic and to be forced to dash out of the meeting-room in front of a multitude of shocked eyes, so I typed out every word of the talk in case my mind froze. When the time came, in my nervousness I read from the notes but did not panic, and all seemed to have gone well until a few days later a remark from one of the ladies in the audience was relayed back to me.

'Ruth Hurst Vose! She's no good. She just reads from notes,' she had told her friends to whom I was due to speak in the next month. I was devastated. I could not deny I had used notes, and I felt inadequate, agoraphobic and a total failure. My first reaction was to give up all ideas of public speaking in the future, but my second reaction was a constructive vow never to rely on notes again. It would have been very easy to give up, using agoraphobia as a valid excuse, but the lady unwittingly did me a service, since it shocked me into throwing away my crutches and going on to be a much better and more confident speaker.

Getting on to an aeroplane for the first time in years inevitably frightened me a great deal. This was a very natural reaction in the circumstances and treating the fear in a practical manner, Jim and I took a trial drive to the airport a week before the flight, noting stopping-off places just in case of panic. This paid off handsomely on the actual day of departure since I had no problems at all on the car journey. I knew I would be frightened of getting my agoraphobic symptoms on the plane so I made sure I had an aisle seat, handy for the toilets, which also helped to ease my mind.

I was fortunate in having a sister-in-law who lived within five minutes' drive of Geneva airport which also helped to make my first holiday abroad possible, and after I had explained the practical side of my fears to her—the need to dash to the loo in times of panic—I felt confident enough to see something of Geneva and its surroundings, and to enjoy the novel experience of swimming and sunbathing. I got into the city centre of Geneva for the first time since agoraphobia by crying my fear away. The sight of the *jet d'eau*, which I had thought I should never see again in my lifetime,

completely overwhelmed me, with the released feeling effectively
flooding away my fear.

The question preoccupying most agoraphobic readers at this
point will undoubtedly be—did I panic during the period of my
new freedom? The answer is that I did panic now and again but
it was either inevitable in the healing process (I would panic whenever I went beyond my rapidly increasing stress threshold), or it
was entirely my own fault when I should have known better.

I have always had a tendency to work myself to a standstill as
long as there is any energy left in me and I did just the same as I
worked through my agoraphobia, with the inevitable result that I
would suddenly hit my stress threshold and my agoraphobic symptoms would move in immediately. After one of these panic bouts I
would be left bewildered, thinking that I was just as badly agoraphobic as before—until I totted up what I had been doing and
realised just how far I had been pushing myself.

Logic plays very little part in one's feelings as one gets close to
the point of recovery. I became even more angry about the unfairness of my agoraphobia as it dissipated, and even more resentful of my symptoms as they appeared less and less. I would blame
the Institute for the slightest re-emergence of my symptoms, even
thinking that 'It hasn't worked!' as I felt a bit hairy for a few
moments on the New York State highway over 3,000 miles from
home. Agoraphobes remain impossible people to the end.

Peter knew precisely what was going on and put up with my
tantrums with equanimity, since he knew that the anger, im-
patience and intolerance of my agoraphobia would help me reach
complete cure in the shortest possible time. I knew I would have
no rest until I was completely better and 99 per cent was simply
not good enough for me. At one point very close to recovery, the
storms inside me made me turn on Peter and make vicious personal
attacks because I blamed him for everything I was going through,
but fortunately he knew it was all a therapeutic blow-out, and our
mutual liking and respect survived unscathed through the traumas.

A final warning note must be sounded on the concept of full
recovery. Although I am not an agoraphobe and never can be

again, since the basic causes have been irreversibly removed, very occasionally I can still get a mild attack of agoraphobic symptoms through overworking or through some undue stress.

The symptoms neither worry me nor incapacitate me because I know precisely why they happen. In fact, if I had not been an agoraphobe, I would never recognise them for what they are and would put them down to 'feeling a bit off colour', 'feeling a bit run down' or any of the other vague reasons put forward—quite correctly—by the rest of humanity to explain a slight feeling of malaise.

The reason I do not give exact descriptions of the exercises which were designed for me by the Institute is that as every agoraphobe is different, no two exercise programmes are likely to be exactly the same. In addition, there would be a very real danger of sufferers trying things out on their own which would be useless and possibly harmful, since it is absolutely essential that the tests and exercises are directed and worked out individually by the doctor or therapist for each patient to be truly effective.

The new approach of the Institute for Neuro-Physiological Psychology—so called because its research deals with human beings in all these aspects—gave me the necessary breakthrough to get rid of my agoraphobia completely. Whether its techniques can do the same for other agoraphobes and what implications its methods have for the wider field of medicine will be considered in the next chapter.

REFERENCES

Benedikt, M. (1870). Uber Platzschwindel. *Allgemeiner Wierner Medizinische Zeitung*, 15, 488.

Sauvages, F. B. de (1770–1). *Nosologie Methodique*, Volume 2, pp. 606–617. Translated by J. Nicolas. Herissant, Paris.

Chapter 8

The Wider Implications

Nearly two and a half thousand years ago Hippocrates wrote: 'It ought to be generally known that the source of our pleasure, merriment, laughter and amusement, as of our grief, pain, anxiety and tears, is none other than the brain. ... It is the brain too which is the seat of madness and delirium, of the fears and frights which assail us often by night, but sometimes even by day; it is there where lies the cause of insomnia and sleep-walking, of thoughts which will not come, forgotten duties and eccentricities. All such things result from an unhealthy condition of the brain.'

In the early years of this century Sigmund Freud said he believed that one day someone would find an organic or physical basis for neuroses.

Both the 'father of medicine' and the 'father of psychoanalysis' are at last being proved right in their predictions with the seeds of research into this area at last bearing rich fruit. Work in this fascinating field is taking place on the Continent, in South Africa and in America, although little interest has been shown in the rather more conservative ranks of British medicine.

The majority of research into minimal brain dysfunction (MBD) has taken place in the USA with major contributions being made by Leopold Bellak, S. D. Clements, S. I. Greenspan, Peter Hartocollis of the C. F. Menninger Memorial Hospital, Kansas, H. B. Mann, R. S. Paine, D. M. and S. A. Ross, and P. H. Wender. In 1979, the results of an important American symposium into minimal brain dysfunction were published, presenting solid evidence for an organic basis to neuroses, where emotional disorders were proved to be secondary to underlying MBD factors (Bellak, 1979).

Minimal brain dysfunction has aroused considerable interest in

Sweden with the greatest contribution coming from Bengt Hagberg of Gothenburg's East Hospital, but none of these researchers has been able to do anything about curing minimal brain dysfunction, perhaps with the exception of Miriam Bender of Purdue University. Dr Bender found a symmetrical tonic neck reflex in over 75 per cent of the learning-disabled children she examined. She drew up a remedial programme for the STNR but not for any other primitive reflexes. (The presence of a symmetrical tonic neck reflex can be a serious obstacle to learning to crawl and will result in later problems in movement and coordination.) (Bender, 1976.)

The Chester Institute for Neuro-Physiological Psychology's unique achievement in this field is that besides testing for dysfunction, it can also measure the percentage of dysfunction and it can remediate or cure it. Its findings and strictly scientific approach have been welcomed with great interest in Sweden, which now has over 200 professionals, including psychologists, psychiatrists, paediatric physicians, speech therapists and teachers in special education, trained in the detection and remediation of organic brain dysfunction (the Institute's more precise definition of minimal brain dysfunction). Sweden's interest is centred on children with learning difficulties, with OBD (organic brain dysfunction) therapy now being available within the state education system from the Arctic Circle to the south of the country. Its application is currently being extended to adults with emotional problems with over 20 psychiatrists and psychologists already using the methods systematically in their practices.

The Swedish Institute for Neuro-Physiological Psychology was established in Gothenburg in 1977 and is run by child psychologist Catherina Johannesson and psychologist Robert Jerdén, who concentrates on adults with organic brain dysfunction. Peter Blythe, Director of the Chester Institute, has given many training courses in OBD therapy to professionals in Sweden, with the first courses for teachers and therapists in Britain being given in 1980. Postgraduate pilot studies into organic factors underlying adult illiteracy in Sweden have already produced significant results (Andréasson, and Lissdaniels, 1979).

Over 500 children with learning difficulties and over 400 adults who have been resistant to other therapies have been treated for organic brain dysfunction by the Chester Institute's remedialists with a success which has sometimes verged on the spectacular. There has been considerable success with long-term clinical depressives, whose symptoms simply vanish after being treated for their organic problems. After OBD therapy, children who could not read began reading without any additional remedial teaching, children whose reading age was significantly retarded have made dramatic and measurable improvements without any additional tutoring, and dyslexics have lost their learning disability (Blythe and McGlown, 1978).

It should be emphasised strongly that not all children with learning problems and not all adults with neuroses have organic brain dysfunction, but for those who do remediation has contributed greatly to the remission of their symptoms.

There is much discussion in modern psychiatric medicine on the possible genetic transmission of neurosis, where problems are inherited through the family. From the research carried out at the Chester Institute between 30 and 50 per cent of patients with organic brain dysfunction appear to have a hereditary factor; otherwise dysfunction is caused by an insult or attack on the central nervous system, usually when the patient was very young and the brain and central nervous system was maturing. A small genetic factor in some agoraphobic cases is indicated by a study which found it more prevalent in identical than in fraternal twins (Carey, 1978). Other research has shown that there is a possible genetic factor, including a survey of 55 agoraphobes where 84 per cent could identify a close relative who suffered from a primary affective (emotional) disorder (Bowen and Kohout, 1979).

Happily the Institute has found that it is possible to remediate dysfunctions even where there has been genetic transmission, but the home programme invariably takes longer to be effective.

Before looking at agoraphobia and OBD therapy in detail, I shall first give a more exact definition of organic brain dysfunction and the importance of primitive reflexes in the development of human beings, as well as a description of the testing and remediation procedure used for all OBD problems.

ORGANIC BRAIN DYSFUNCTION

The origin of the term organic brain dysfunction has already been explained on p. 138, but further clarification of its difference from minimal brain dysfunction is necessary to put it into a proper scientific context.

Organic brain dysfunction means the presence of three things in a human being. The first of these is *aberrant motor patterns of development*, which include the presence of *primitive reflexes* which should have disappeared in early infancy, but which have persisted into later life beyond their expectancy. For instance, a child who has not developed a transformed tonic neck reflex will never go through the stages of crawling and creeping properly, and will have lost out on a vital stage in neural development.

The second area for OBD is *cross-laterality or marked ambiguity of laterality*. Cross-laterality, or the arrested establishment of cerebral dominance, is where a person might be right-handed and left-footed or right-eyed and left-handed. Cross-dominancy has been associated with a vulnerability to physical stress and added to other OBD factors can place a person psychologically at risk. Ambiguity of laterality occurs where a person might be right-eyed for sighting long distances and left-eyed for sighting short distances, or he might hold a cricket bat with his left hand but throw the cricket ball with his right hand. Quite frequently the non-dominant hand will have more natural dexterity than it should have if proper laterality was established.

The third OBD area is *visual perceptual problems*. This is nothing to do with sight problems which can be corrected by opticians' lenses, but has everything to do with how the eye muscles work, and whether the eyes work in concert sending signals back to the visual cortex of the brain. Perceptual problems include increased physiological nystagmus (involuntary oscillations of the eyeball); defective eye muscle movements which can result in the eyes not yoking together; latent strabismus (squint), both divergent when the eye turns out, and convergent when the eye turns in; the inability to ignore irrelevant stimuli, where a person becomes 'stimulus bound'; and poor scanning ability. The most frequent perceptual dysfunction appears in the area of *visual-motor integration difficulties* where there is a marked lack of eye–hand coordination. In other words the hand finds it difficult to carry out what the eye and brain demand.

The second and third areas of OBD are the direct results of the presence of primitive reflexes in the first area and a person must have difficulties in all three areas before he is classified as having organic brain dysfunction.

THE IMPORTANCE OF PRIMITIVE REFLEXES

The concept of primitive reflexes in human beings will be very new to most people, although most of us will be familiar with the doctor's rubber hammer tapping just below the kneecap to try and raise a reflexive kick during a medical check-up. Yet these reflexes have been the subject of detailed study during the past century by neurophysiologists, physiologists, neurologists, paediatricians, physical therapists, occupational therapists, and others interested in cerebral palsy.

Western medicine is only just beginning to understand the clinical importance not only of the persistence of such reflexes, which are supposed to disappear or become transformed in the early years of life, but also of the more qualitative aspects of their presence.

In our everyday movements we are not conscious of which individual muscles we are using, nor can we voluntarily direct what each muscle should do while we are moving about. Most of our voluntary movements are automatic and outside consciousness, and it is the central nervous system utilising the 'old brain' (deep grey matter) which maintains our posture and equilibrium. Damage to the central nervous system results in abnormal coordination of muscle action.

Normal babies are born with numerous primitive reflexes because of the unrestrained influence of the 'old brain', which contains the centres for these reflexes. The 'old brain' centres include the brainstem, cerebellum, midbrain and basal ganglia. It is the 'new brain', the cerebral cortical mantle, which inhibits and transforms these primitive reflexes so that during normal development they are integrated into more functional postural and voluntary motor responses. If these primitive reflexes for some reason fail to disappear or be transformed, the various deep grey matter responses (primitive reflexes) are a signal for possible brain dysfunction and motor impairment.

In her study of abnormal postural reflex activity caused by brain lesions in children, Berta Bobath of the Western Cerebral Palsy Centre, London, points out that these postural reflexes and their harmonious interaction form the background of normal voluntary movements and skills, and that without their full development and integration normal motor activities can not be expected (Bobath, 1978).

Put very simply, if the reflexes of childhood which are suited to survival as a baby are not transformed into adult reflexes which are necessary for our proper functioning as an adult, we are going to be in trouble both emotionally and physically. It has been found that if more than two primitive reflexes are still with us as adults, we are much more prone to stress and the disorders these bring.

The Chester Institute's remediation programme is a form of reflex patterning. It imposes motor patterns of feedback to the brain which allow the patient to return developmentally to the stage where certain reflexes failed to become modified and transformed appropriately. Reintegration of corrected reflexes can then occur, which in turn promotes more total neurological integration and concomitant emotional harmony in the individual.

TESTING AND REMEDIATION FOR OBD

It is always nice to know what to expect when going for any new treatment, so the following general guidelines are given for both patients and their doctors or therapists.

A patient who has been referred or who comes voluntarily to the Chester Institute or to other OBD therapists will have an initial consultation where he will be put through a screening questionnaire irrespective of his presenting problems.

If the questionnaire indicates that his problems are not due to organic brain dysfunction but are purely emotionally-based, the patient will be recommended to take appropriate psychotherapeutic or other treatment.

If the questionnaire reveals sufficient evidence for possible organic brain dysfunction he will be asked to make an appointment for a diagnostic session which will last between four and five and a half hours. Here he will be examined neurologically for gross muscle coordination, fine muscle coordination, the presence of primitive reflexes, visual perceptual difficulties and visual-motor integration difficulties. He will also be put through an emotional screening to see if there is a low stress tolerance and whether he has been unresponsive to previous treatment (in other words whether he is a recidivist). If organic brain dysfunction is found, an exact measurement of the percentage of the difficulty of functioning is taken so that subsequent improvement can be monitored precisely.

Three weeks after he has been through the diagnostic programme the patient will receive a letter telling him that his report is ready, and asking him to make an appointment. Unlike the general medical or psychological professions, the patient, as well as the doctor, receives a copy of the report, which is usually between 12 and 14 pages long. Because it is written in technical language an Institute psychologist will go through the report with the patient explaining all the details.

The next step is for the patient to receive a home programme based on the OBD factors which have been located. He will see an

Institute remedialist who will give him a home programme and spend a couple of hours showing how the exercises are to be done. The programme which lasts between 20 and 30 minutes has to be carried out by the patient in his own home once a day for the next seven weeks. After that period he will return to the Institute for a review.

The seven weeks' review fulfils a very important purpose. It should be possible to measure some improvement even after this short time, but if there is no remission of the patient's percentage of dysfunctions the Institute remedialist knows that one of three things is happening: the patient has been doing the exercises incorrectly; the patient has not been doing the exercise programme every day; or a reflex has been missed which is preventing the home programme from working.

Providing everything is going well, the Institute will see the patient for further reviews every 13 weeks until the neurological dysfunction is well within the normal level. On the Institute's scale of measurement this would mean 30 per cent for older adults (40 years plus), between 20 and 25 per cent for young adults (25 to 40 years old), and 15 per cent for children.

Because some patients have had their emotional problems for so long, the Institute will recommend that they have contact with their general practitioner, psychiatrist or analyst while they are undergoing the OBD programme. OBD therapy does not necessarily replace other therapies and in many cases is used with them. Some children and adults will regress emotionally while doing the exercise programme, and they will also need psychotherapeutic or drug support.

Critics of the home programme may say that it could be something of a placebo—giving the patient a series of help-yourself tasks coupled with a new belief system could be sufficient on its own to bring about remission in a number of cases.

Although it is undoubtedly pleasant to be able to do something so concrete towards one's recovery, there is no other placebo effect from the exercises. Indeed, the Institute has found that when patients stop doing their exercises because they have experienced some remission in their symptoms, improvement stops immediately and their symptoms have returned. This is because the patients have not carried through the programme to the point where a real reduction in their dysfunctions has been achieved, so the basic faults begin to reassert themselves. Once they recommence their exercises their symptoms again begin to ease until they finally disappear for good (Blythe, 1978).

Details of the screening and diagnostic programme are given in Blythe and McGlown's *An Organic Basis for Neuroses and Educational Difficulties* (1979) and details of the remediation exercises are given in *The Clinician's Handbook for the Detection and Remediation of Organic Brain Dysfunction* (Insight Publications, Chester, 1980) written by the same authors for professionals who have completed a course in OBD therapy.

AGORAPHOBIA AND OBD

Peter Blythe and David McGlown's methods at the Chester Institute have certainly worked for me, but equally importantly they have worked for many other people. Although they have no specific programme devoted to agoraphobes, the second area of their research, which concentrates on adults who have been resistant to other therapies, has produced some remarkable results in the agoraphobic field.

Over 400 adults who have suffered from emotional disorders for an average of seven years have now been treated at Chester for organic brain dysfunction, and among these have been over 70 agoraphobes on whom the following observations are based.

From Peter and David's research it would appear there are two distinct types of agoraphobia. The first is the purely psychological type, where there is a definite psychological phobic fear that something disastrous is going to happen when the person goes out. A good example is the case of an agoraphobic woman who came to a therapist absolutely terrified that she was going to die. Under hypnosis she revealed that everything which had happened to her throughout her life had chronologically happened her mother at the same age. As she was now approaching the age when her mother died she had become agoraphobic. Once the therapist had helped her to see that there was no genetic reason for her dying, and that she was not her mother, her agoraphobia disappeared completely.

A severely agoraphobic young woman could not even hazard a guess why she was frightened to go outside her front door. All she knew was that once she was outside she suffered extreme panic and was sure that something terrible was going to happen to her. Under hypno-analysis she recalled a previously repressed memory of when she had found she was pregnant shortly after the birth of one of her children and had felt she could not cope. In an attempt to terminate her pregnancy she had used a folk-lore method to produce an abortion which was unsuccessful, but she had a miscarriage some weeks later. She was full of guilt at the loss of her unborn child and saw it as God's way of punishing her for the 'sin' she had committed. As a result she wiped out all conscious memory of the attempted abortion and only remembered the loss of the fetus. Once the repressed memory and its associated emotions had been resurrected, the woman realised why she could not leave her house —she unconsciously felt that God would use the opportunity to punish her further. When she could face her action and she realised that it was not so very dreadful, her agoraphobic symptoms disappeared (Blythe, 1975).

The Institute has found that these purely emotional agoraphobia sufferers form about 25 per cent of the agoraphobic population, and generally speaking they will respond to any type of therapy. It is interesting to note that the success rate of all previous therapies rarely exceeds 30 per cent for a complete cure which ties in with the Institute's findings.

As the agoraphobia is due to purely emotional factors and learned behaviour where the patient is frightened to go out, it will respond to whichever therapy the sufferer finds most useful. Psychoanalysts will have success with emotional agoraphobes by helping them to recognise and resolve their emotional conflicts so that they are once more free to go out. Behavioural therapy will also be successful as it teaches the agoraphobe a new behavioural attitude or conditioning. Hypnosis will be very useful to some people by helping them to come into contact with their unconscious conflicts, and facing and resolving them. Drugs will also have a good chance of success by lowering the internal excitation level so that the person learns to cope once more and develops a new learned behavioural pattern.

But the majority of agoraphobes come under the second category defined by the Institute, which is those who are likely to have a physical basis for their neuroses. They will have a whole series of difficulties in functioning, particularly in the vestibular and perceptual areas, and it is their efforts to compensate for this which lead to agoraphobia. (See p. 141.)

Neurologists have suggested that people who are deeply neurotic will have balance problems, but the Institute believes that this is 'putting the cart before the horse' and that it works the other way round—people who have balance problems are prone to become neurotic. Agoraphobes have been found to be particularly prone to problems within the vestibular or balancing apparatus, which under pressure from external stressors will reach a point where the basic faults begin to show themselves.

Indeed, from their decade of research, Peter and David have found that people with organic brain dysfunction have a lower stress tolerance and are more likely to be affected by emotional and physical stress. People can compensate for their OBD quite unconsciously since they have been doing it all their lives. Providing the stress level stays below a certain tolerance level they can continue to function and only under stress do the dysfunctions begin to show.

Agoraphobes with OBD problems are generally found to be 'stimulus bound' which means they are unable to ignore irrelevant movements going on around them. Because their eyes are constantly picking up movement they cannot tolerate too many people or too much action around them. They become overwhelmed by the barrage of stimuli to the eyes, which is why shopping at busy times can be a most difficult and dizzying experience.

Although agoraphobes are likely to have other OBD problems including aberrant reflexes, the balance mechanism faults and the 'stimulus bound' perceptual problems have been found to be the most common difficulties. They are basic physical faults which have always been there, and since OBD patients are typically hypersensitive in more than one area of their functioning, they are particularly prone to stress.

Adult OBD patients have been able to compensate for many years for their various dysfunctions, but the law of compensation is that they have to pay a price at another level of functioning which is exacted most often at the emotional level.

For the agoraphobe, the first time outside stress factors reach a pitch where his compensatory mechanisms break down, his perceptual and balancing problems will suddenly reveal themselves in a quite frightening manner. Utterly unconscious of his OBD problems, he will find for no apparent reason that he feels he is going to fall over, that he is about to faint, his eyes begin to play tricks and he finds he cannot focus them properly. As in sea sickness, this in turn brings on nausea and the desire to vomit and defaecate.

The person cannot explain why he has had this attack which bears every resemblance to panic. The first time it happens it frightens him because he cannot understand it, which increases his internal excitation level. Not unnaturally, the next time he goe. out the tension level actually goes up, so the same thing happens again only faster, and very soon the true agoraphobic reaction sets in.

From this it is easy to see that agoraphobia is a natural progression. The physical factors remain undetected but can be activated by stress, pleasant or unpleasant; the eyes and balancing mechanisms are then no longer able to function properly, nausea and 'sea sickness' symptoms set in, and then fear of fear develops since the person cannot understand what is happening to them.

What is organic in the beginning very quickly becomes psychological, with fear of loss of control becoming paramount.

Various therapies have assisted agoraphobes suffering from
organic brain dysfunction to overcome their symptoms to some
degree, but they do not solve the basic physical problems. Drugs
and hypnotism help by lowering the stress level so the person can
compensate once more for their dysfunctions. Behavioural therapy
teaches the patient to have a higher stress tolerance, so again they
can compensate for much longer and their balancing and perceptual
problems will not reappear within that extra boundary. However,
in these and other therapies, if stress manages to reach beyond the
new tolerance levels the symptoms will reappear again quite
naturally.

The mystery of agoraphobia put into this context begins to
make a lot of sense. Agoraphobia can no longer be seen as a demon
who for no apparent reason takes possession of an unsuspecting
person, changing his whole life into one of permanent fear. The
baffling question of 'Why has it happened to me and not to other
people?' is now answered in a very logical way. Once the organic
or physical basis for agoraphobia has been worked out for the
majority of individuals it is possible to see from where those 'out
of the blue' attacks appear. Where there is a concentration of irregular movement, noise and bright light, the stimulus can get
too much and the central nervous system will 'blow a fuse'. Like
many agoraphobes, I knew that if I merely became overtired I was
much more likely to get an attack of agoraphobic symptoms, since
my system had gone into a state of overload.

The Institute has found that once agoraphobes who have lost
the ability to compensate for underlying organic brain dysfunction
have been put on to a remediation programme, the vast majority
get better, and it describes its success rate as 'very high'.

The agoraphobe is put through the testing and remediation pro-
cedures in exactly the same way as all other patients. The initial
screening will tell him beyond doubt whether his problems are
purely emotional or whether they are due to basic organic faults.

If he is a psychological type of agoraphobe, the emotional screening developed by the Institute will help to isolate the core of his problems so that the most appropriate therapy for him can be worked out. This is valuable for both patient and doctor since many people can enter therapies which are not right for their emotional condition and will not respond.

For the agoraphobe with organic brain dysfunction, his direction is clear. His biggest difficulty will be completing the 30 minutes' exercise programme every day which can get very boring indeed. My advice is to be completely bloody-minded about it. Set yourself a time where you know you are normally not disturbed, and quite regardless of sickness, visitors, telephones ringing or the demands of work or the family, get them done. This is one area where I allowed full rein to my neuroticism and obsessive-compulsiveness so that I never missed my exercises once!

In addition to the remediation programme, the Institute has found it necessary to take some OBD agoraphobes into psycho-therapy to help resolve their emotional fears. Even though their neuroses are secondary, since they are the direct result of physical dysfunctions, psycho-counselling is sometimes necessary to help them to recognise what is happening to them so that they will lose their fear of the fear.

There are some failures, although these form a very small percentage of the total. Some patients fail to see the significance of the remediation exercises and find them monotonous, and because they see no initial benefit they tend to give up very easily. Another area of failure both with emotional and organic agoraphobes is with those who get massive secondary gains from their condition. At an unconscious level they realise that if they lose their agoraphobic symptoms, horrible though they are, they will then have to face the reality of their relationships, and therefore the symptoms are necessary to them. (See p. 86.)

SHORT- AND LONG-TERM PROSPECTS

Some doctors and psychotherapists are already using organic brain dysfunction screening methods in Britain, and around 1,000

patients who have previously been resistant to treatment have gone
through the OBD remediation programme with a very high level
of success. But compared to Sweden there are very few OBD therapists in this country and the next five years should see what kind
of response the British Medical Association and the National
Health Service will make to this new research.

Reactions from doctors have already ranged from welcoming the
work as the biggest breakthrough since Louis Pasteur to dismissing
it as 'a complete load of rubbish' since primitive reflexes 'cannot
exist' in adults! Even if doctors accept that the primitive reflexes
are there, the fact that they can be remediated will be a difficult
pill to swallow.

The proof of the pudding lies in the eating, and it is to be hoped
that the sceptics will examine the overwhelming evidence that this
can be done consistently well. Perhaps the most powerful weapon
in the medical armoury is total indifference, which can kill new
ideas by simply ignoring them. If this were to happen, I feel the
sceptics would be responsible for the biggest step backwards this
century in the treatment of neuroses, abandoning many psychiatric
patients and ordinary individuals to a fate which need not be theirs.

Doctors and psychologists may see the new approach as an attack on their methods, but this is certainly not the case. OBD
therapy treats the basic cause of many neuroses but certainly not
all, and purely emotional sufferers must be treated by conventional
methods. As has already been pointed out, OBD therapy is usually
used concomitantly with other treatments, accelerating their effectiveness, so there is little danger of any redundancies in existing
treatments, and their chances of success are much increased.

The other 'threat' from the new approach is that it crosses professional demarcation lines. OBD therapists are testing for primitive reflexes which is the work of either the paediatric physician
or paediatric neurologist; and they are checking on cross-laterality
and perceptual problems which is normally the work of the
psychologist.

In practical terms this is bound to cause professional problems,
but before the hatchets come out it should be pointed out that this

type of difficulty is already being tackled successfully in other parts of the western world. The USA's John F. Kennedy Institute for Handicapped Children has already pioneered the training of a new breed of interdisciplinary paediatrician. It has found that a minimum of two to three years' training in a multidisciplinary academic setting is necessary before doctors can comfortably cross traditional demarcation lines. Its present syllabus requires the cooperation between physicians (developmental paediatricians) and paramedical professionals (physical therapists) who use each other's techniques towards the goal of development paediatrics which encompass the whole patient (Capute et al, 1978).

Peter Blythe's view is that the general practitioner could use the screening procedure on patients with emotional problems who appear to have a low stress tolerance and who have not responded to drugs or other treatment. Nurses inside group practices or physiotherapists could be taught to be diagnosticians or remedialists for organic brain dysfunction without causing any extra cost to the National Health Service.

The number of patients which a doctor would screen would be small, but the saving in drugs and time would be comparatively large since these patients will be the ones who would normally be on drugs or other treatments for years, occupying the doctor's time year in, year out, with no appreciable improvement.

OBD therapy is strictly a scientific method for isolating those people who are stress prone, but who can be made stress-proof to a greater or lesser degree. The potential benefits to patients, doctors and the National Health Service in terms of smaller drugs bills, cutting down on long-term treatments and, most important of all, achieving complete health and cure would appear to be self-evident.

REFERENCES

Andréasson, Jarl and Lissdaniels, Britt. (1979). A *Field Study of Adults with Reading and Writing Problems from a Neuro-Physiological Viewpoint.* Gothenburg University Psychological Institution.

Bellak, Leopold (1979). *Psychiatric Aspects of Minimal Brain Dysfunction in Adults*. Grune and Stratton, New York and London.

Bender, Miriam L. (1976). *The Bender-Purdue Reflex Test and Training Manual*. Academic Therapy Publications, San Rafael, California.

Blythe, Peter (1975). *Stress. The Modern Sickness*, p. 19–20. (first published as 'Stress Disease. The Growing Plague'. Arthur Barker, 1973) Pan Books, London and Sydney.

Blythe, Peter (1978). Minimal Brain Dysfunction and the Treatment of Psycho-Neuroses. *Journal of Psychosomatic Research*, 22 (4), 247–255.

Blythe, Peter and McGlown, David J. (1978). *Neurological Disorganisation, Dyslexia and Learning Difficulties*. Paper given to the Symposium on 'Dyslexia: Its Diagnosis and Treatment', Manchester, February 15–17.

Bobath, Berta (1978). *Abnormal Postural Reflex Activity caused by Brain Lesions*, p. 103. Second edition. William Heinemann Medical Books, London.

Bowen, R. C. and Kohout, J. (1979). The Relationship between Agoraphobia and Primary Affective Disorders. *Canadian Journal of Psychiatry*, 24, 317–322.

Carey, G. (1978). Ph. D. dissertation. University of Minnesota.

Capute, A. J., Accardo, P. J., Vining, E. P. G., Rubenstein, J. E. and Harryman, S. (1978). *Primitive Reflex Profile*, pp. xiii–xiv. University Park Press, Baltimore, London and Tokyo.

Chapter 9

Conclusion

My agoraphobia began as a story of panic on a scale unimaginable by even the most skilled horror-movie maker. I began by considering that agoraphobia was a monster which tormented me in a way I would not wish on any other human being. I end by admitting that agoraphobia has brought me a richness in life which I never knew existed, that it has given me one of the most fascinating experiences possible, and that, despite the nightmare, I would not have missed it for the world.

The story would have been a very different one had I not been cured, and I should have joined the pathetic ranks of other agoraphobic writers such as David and Professor Leonard. If they could only have lived to see this decade their stories and lives might have been very different. Being 'better' is not just being rid of agoraphobic symptoms, because in the process of being cured the personality has grown and matured as well. My pre-agoraphobic days bear no resemblance at all to my post-agoraphobic experience and my first 30 years of life might as well belong to another person for the little relevance they bear to me now. I am no longer a prisoner of the past but merely a product of it.

The distinguished American psychologist Carl R. Rogers described life at its best being a process of 'becoming'. From the static, frozen world of the agoraphobe, my life is indeed a flowing, changing process where nothing is fixed and will forever be 'becoming'. As my fear of the world decreased, both my outer and inner vision expanded, bringing back the delight and intensity of colour, sound and touch which I fleetingly felt as a child. I no longer wish to be like others nor do I seek their approbation. I am happy being me. I see myself and other people for the reality of what we are, and love others better for it. It has taken me nearly half a lifetime to find out that until I can love myself I cannot love my fellow men, and that true love means simple acceptance.

As an interested and highly involved bystander, Jim considers that the single most important factor in getting well from agoraphobia is the will to get better or, at its most basic, the will to live. There is as much difference between living and existing as there is between heaven and hell. There is a world of difference again between being taught to cope with life and being cured. Having a lively sense of humour, an interesting and fulfilling job, and one good friend to whom you can talk are also practical factors I would never underestimate in winning the agoraphobic fight.

Even though OBD therapy has made the breakthrough in establishing the major causes and successfully treating agoraphobia, this book will have shown that agoraphobes have found many and diverse routes towards the ultimate goal of recovery. Behavioural therapy, drugs, spiritual healing, hypnotism, acupuncture and the rest—they all have something positive to offer the agoraphobe and it is up to the individual to get out there and find out what is best for him.

Better treatment and facilities will only result from agitation at grass-roots level, so that politicians and medical authorities can no longer ignore the necessity of channelling the most basic resource into this area. There is not much glamour or incentive for doctors and psychologists who do decide to specialise in agoraphobia or other mental disorders, and it is high time that they received the same money and kudos given to those specialising in the equally widespread problems of cancer and heart disease.

Ultimately, one must hope for the emergence of a society which is less stress-prone, where people can be themselves without interference from others, and where agoraphobia and other stress disorders which are the hallmarks of modern civilisation will disappear into the past where they really belong.

Statistics on Agoraphobia

Statistics on agoraphobia, how many suffer from it, the type of person, the symptoms, the success rate of treatments and so on, abound in learned articles. A computer scan of all articles written in English on the treatment of phobias and agoraphobia in particular, in the last 15 years, produced well over 500 books and articles, covering everything from the treatment of agoraphobia by induced anger, to the many problems of the husbands of agoraphobic women. It is disappointing that so little progress has been made in the treatment of agoraphobia when so much energy has been expended in writing and researching into the problem.

Although statistics are meaningless as far as the treatment of individuals are concerned, they do present a more global picture of the problem of agoraphobia which helps to put it into some general perspective. It is important to bear in mind while scanning the following statistics that agoraphobes are as different from each other as every human being, no two ever being quite alike.

AGORAPHOBIA IN THE COMMUNITY

There has been a marked lack of empirically based information on the prevalence of phobias in adults. Few of the early studies differentiated phobias from other neuroses, although exceptions were Lemkau, Tietze and Cooper's (1942) study and Hollingshead and Redlich's (1958) research which both estimated that 0.5 per cent per 1,000 of the population were phobia sufferers. A number of studies in the 1960s involving college students are unreliable since the subjects reporting severe fears were not incapacitated in their everyday functioning to the extent that they sought treatment.

Agras, Sylvester and Oliveau conducted one of the few systematic surveys in 1969 when 325 subjects and 50 phobic subjects were interviewed in Great Burlington, Vermont. As the sample was so small (1 : 193 sample of the population) the results must be regarded as provisional, but they showed that an estimated 77 per 1,000 of the population were suffering from phobias, although severely disabling phobias were estimated at only 2.2 per 1,000. Although agoraphobia formed 50 per cent of clinical cases for the two psychiatrists, its incidence in the general population was estimated at 6.3 per 1,000. This meant that in a small town with a population of 100,000 one might expect to find 630 people suffering from agoraphobia, and 7,700 suffering from general phobias.

Isaac Marks reported in the same year that the commonest clinical phobia encountered at Maudsley Hospital was agoraphobia, forming 60 per cent of clinical cases (Marks, 1969). From this and the previous study, it would appear that over half the phobic cases encountered in clinical practice are likely to be agoraphobic in nature.

From surveys completed on the frequency of phobic disorders in psychiatric practice up to 1969, though phobic symptoms might be present in 20 per cent of psychiatric patients, phobic disorders were found in fewer than three per cent of all cases seen in America and England (Marks, 1969). The number is in fact larger than appears, agoraphobia being acknowledged to be the commonest and the most distressing phobia seen by psychiatrists.

The most significant contribution to our present knowledge of the prevalence and nature of agoraphobia in Britain today was made by the National Survey of Agoraphobics which commenced in 1973. Four years later the results were reported by Lawrence E. Burns, Principal Clinical Psychologist of Birch Hill Hospital, Rochdale, and G. L. Thorpe of the Mount Desert Island Family Counselling Service, Bar Harbor, Maine, USA, in volume 5 of the *Journal of International Medical Research*.

Exactly 963 sufferers were contacted for the survey through radio, television and newspaper publicity, plus the help of the major phobic organisations—The Phobics Society (Manchester),

The Open Door (London), the Thanet Group Phobic Trust (Kent), and Merseyside and Yorkshire groups. Up to this survey the number of agoraphobia sufferers in this country was estimated at 300,000. Now it has been shown that agoraphobia is a significant community problem with 10 persons per 1,000—that is around 500,000 in the United Kingdom, suffering to a greater or lesser degree from agoraphobia—and that is without counting the millions suffering from other phobic conditions.

The two main phobic organisations, The Open Door Association (TODA) and The Phobics Society, each have over 5,000 members to date (although there is some overlapping). Since the formation of The Open Door Association (TODA), the original phobics organisation, in 1965, it has helped between 40,000 and 50,000 people and the results of a survey of 1,200 TODA members were reported by Marks in *Fears and Phobias* (1969).

The results of another large survey of 528 agoraphobic men and women she had treated in Great Britain were published by the Australian doctor Claire Weekes in volume 2 of the *British Medical Journal*, 1973.

SEX INCIDENCE

That women form the majority of agoraphobes is a fact which has been statistically proved many times. At least two-thirds of agoraphobes seen by psychiatrists in Britain and America are women. Recently, the National Survey of Agoraphobics revealed that 88.16 per cent of the people taking part were women and Weekes found 91 per cent of the patients she surveyed were women.

On the face of it, this huge majority may seem odd, since sex incidence in other neurotic disorders can be quite different—to use a small example, four-fifths of patients with writer's cramp are men. Almost undoubtedly the social and environmental conditions for women directly cause this large figure. It has also been found that women are more likely to report their fears than men (Wilson,

1967), and that during periods of high arousability (for example, the few days preceding menstruation) women are perhaps more prone to acquiring aversive responses (Asso and Beech, 1975).

AGE OF ONSET

It is rare for agoraphobia to start in childhood, and it usually begins in young adult life between 18 and 35 years old. The mean age of onset was found to be 24 years at Maudsley Hospital, and 28 years in The Open Door sample of 1,200 agoraphobics throughout Britain. Weekes found the majority of her patients became ill in their twenties and thirties, and the National Survey confirmed that the mean age of onset was 28.02 years (standard deviation 10.35 years).

Burns and Thorpe reported a statistically significant difference between the mean age of onset for men and women: 28.51 (standard deviation 10.30 years) for women, and 24.25 years (standard deviation 10.00 years) for men. Only 9.3 per cent of the National Survey got agoraphobia below the age of 16 years, with a rare 13.2 per cent developing the condition at 40 or more.

Agoraphobia follows the pattern of anxiety states which have a similar range of age of onset to the agoraphobic syndrome.

PANIC

Burns and Thorpe noted that acute panic is one of the most distressing aspects of agoraphobia. The National Survey gave revealing data on what agoraphobes considered would be the worst thing that could happen during a panic. 98.4 per cent reported a first fear, and 35.4 per cent reported a second fear.

A fear of fainting or collapsing was most frequently cited (37.9 per cent, first fear; 15.8 per cent, second fear). On the face of it this seems odd since it is well established that agoraphobes rarely faint when panicking, but good reasons for this apparently ground-less fear have now been pinpointed. (See pp. 141, 160–1.)

The National Survey also showed that fear of dying is a major dread of many agoraphobes (13.2 per cent, first fear; 19.7 per cent, second fear). This is frequently caused by an attack of severe pal-pitations during a panic episode, which gives rise to the immediate fear that they are having a heart attack or perhaps a brain haemor-rhage. Fear of a heart attack was itself cited by 4.1 per cent (first fear) and 4 per cent (second fear).

Causing a scene (6.2 per cent, first fear; 25.8 per cent, second fear), and other personal illness (10.4 per cent, first fear; 9.7 per cent, second fear) were the next most significant fears. Becoming mentally ill, inability to get home or to a place of safety, and losing control (e.g. becoming hysterical) averaged around the 7 per cent mark. Loss of memory was the least of the 'worst' fears during panic, scoring only 0.3 per cent (first fear) and 0.9 per cent (second fear).

Buglass et al (1977) found that the most common fear of agora-phobes was the fear of becoming physically ill (fainting, dying, having a heart attack), which tallies well with the National Survey. The fear was often accompanied by concern for causing a public disturbance.

From the results of medication, there would appear to be a pos-sibility that panic and anxiety do not necessarily go together. Klein (1964) found that imipramine was highly effective in de-creasing panic attacks, but had no apparent effect on expectant or anticipatory anxiety. He stressed the obvious role panic plays in causing and maintaining agoraphobia. General anxiety and panic attacks occur in non-agoraphobic anxiety states, but here, once the panic and anxiety are over, the person can readily resume a normal life. This is not so for an agoraphobia sufferer who needs subsequent treatment for his phobias.

Marks observed that anxiety states and agoraphobia can merge and can be given both labels, but at the extreme of divergence, only one or other of the labels is appropriate (Marks, 1969). Some agora-phobes do not complain of much general anxiety.

FAMILY, PERSONALITY AND BACKGROUND

A generally stable family background for agoraphobes has been claimed by various researchers (Terhune, 1949; Roth, 1959; Marks and Gelder, 1965). Marks observed that the stable family background of agoraphobes differs markedly from that of psychopaths, where broken homes are the general rule (Marks, 1965). In Weekes' survey, the large majority of agoraphobes claimed to be happy or passably happy within their present domestic condition.

On the other hand, over-protectiveness on the part of the family was found by Terhune, and Webster (1953) also found that mothers tended to be over-protective, although he was alone in finding that fathers were absent from home rather more than usual. Snaith (1968) found an excess of unstable family backgrounds, and Buglass et al (1977) said that agoraphobes tend to come from anomalous home situations compared to control groups, more frequently featuring step-parents, step-siblings or adopted siblings.

The National Survey examined the mother and father relationships, with 16.1 per cent reporting a distant or very distant relationship with the mother, and nearly 30 per cent similarly with the father. 36.7 per cent felt their mothers were over-protective, 43.1 per cent said their mothers were often over-anxious, with only 11.2 per cent seen as rejecting. On the other hand, 42.9 per cent said their fathers were strict and 32.2 per cent said they were un-affectionate.

Agoraphobes in general are not unusual in intelligence, occupation or education. The Open Door sample confirmed that agoraphobes in Britain are average in education, occupation, income and religious affiliation.

Many agoraphobes tend to have a premorbid personality before they develop agoraphobic symptoms, which has been variously described as soft, anxious, passive, shy and dependent (Marks, 1969). Contrarily agoraphobia certainly has been known to begin in people who are naturally outgoing, active and sociable. It would seem there has been little change since M. Prince noted in 1912 that such phobias 'occur in people of all types and characteristics, amongst the normally self-reliant as well as amongst the timid'.

There is evidence to show that some agoraphobia sufferers come from a background of the same disorder or of other nervous disorders. Marks and Herst (1969) found that 19 per cent of agoraphobes in Britain reported that they had a close relative also suffering from agoraphobia. Roth (1959) and Roberts (1964) found that psychiatric disorder in the family of agoraphobes ranges from 21 per cent to 40 per cent. A comparison between the families of phobics and the families of temporal lobe epileptics was made by Harper and Roth (1962), which showed that the incidence of neurosis in the families of phobics (33 per cent) was significantly higher.

The National Survey showed that at least one in three of the agoraphobia sufferers interviewed had at least one sibling requiring treatment for some nervous disorder. 13.1 per cent reported the father requiring treatment, 28.1 per cent, the mother, and 34.9 per cent, brothers/sisters. Buglass et al (1977) said that 30 per cent of the siblings of agoraphobes had a positive history of psychiatric illness. Bowen and Kohout (1979) found 84 per cent of their patients could identify a close relative with a probable primary affective disorder.

Genetic studies of first-degree relatives and twin studies indicate the presence of a significant genetic component in anxiety neurosis, and this has been borne out to some degree with agoraphobia where it is known to be more prevalent in identical than fraternal twins. (See p. 152.)

CHILDHOOD

On the surface, childhood problems do not appear excessive in agoraphobia sufferers. 75 per cent of Weekes' patients said their childhood was either very happy, happy or passably happy. Only 25 per cent said it had been unhappy.

The National Survey showed that nearly 70 per cent of agoraphobes said their feelings were too easily hurt in childhood. Fears of the dark gained the next highest percentage (45.8 per cent); nightmares, nail biting, slow in making friends, fears about going to school were all around the 30 per cent mark; bedwetting and fears of animals each gained just above 13 per cent, with stammering (3.6 per cent), thumb sucking (6.7 per cent), and trouble with the police (2.1 per cent) achieving the lowest response. 46.8 per cent complained of other unspecified childhood fears.

The questionable value of statistics is spotlighted when the results of a study of the childhood fears of non-psychiatric or 'normal' children (Lapouse and Monk, 1958; 1959) are compared to the above, with a striking resemblance between the incidence of nightmares (28 per cent), bedwetting (17 per cent), stammering (4 per cent), nail biting (27 per cent) and thumb sucking (10 per cent).

The National Survey indicated that more boys than girls suffered from stammering (10 per cent v 3 per cent), were slow in making friends (40.35 per cent v 27.03 per cent), and had trouble with the police (8.77 per cent v 1.19 per cent). However several studies have found an incidence of childhood enuresis (bedwetting), fears and night terrors in phobics of up to 55 per cent (Marks and Gelder, 1965). Harper and Roth in their comparative study between agoraphobes and temporal lobe epileptics found the agoraphobes had a significantly commoner history of childhood phobias.

Childhood clinical problems seem to occur very infrequently. Only 4.2 per cent of cases referred to the Maudsley Hospital Children's Department related to phobic reactions (Marks and Gelder, 1969). A minute 0.7 per cent of over 2,000 children aged 10 or 11 years surveyed for psychiatric disorders in the Isle of Wight had clinically significant and disabling phobias (Rutter, Tizard and Whitmore, 1968).

Childhood fears tend to be transitory and on the whole do not lead to the avoidance of the feared situation, so cannot really be classed as phobias. An exception is school phobia, where the child will try to resist all attempts to get him to school, manifesting psychosomatic (stress induced) illnesses, and refusing all reassurances or coercion to get to school. School phobia, which has some of the marks of agoraphobia, is said to be on the increase, with an estimated 17 per 1,000 children a year suffering from it (Kennedy, 1965). Once established it can become one of the most disabling of childhood emotional disorders. Some adult agoraphobes are known to have suffered from school phobia during childhood and 32.4 per cent of the National Survey reported fears about going to school. As it was much more difficult and socially unacceptable to miss school a decade or so ago, it is possible that it was equally difficult for school phobia to become fully established as it has done in more recent times. In fact there are few records of much aggressive behaviour or truanting by agoraphobes in childhood.

Patients with a history of childhood fears of leaving parents, or fears of the dark or excessive night terrors tend to get agoraphobia and come for treatment 6 to 12 years before other agoraphobic patients (Klein, 1964; Marks, unpublished data). Sufferers can often show an early predisposition to separation anxiety, persistence of infantile dependency and a lack of self-identity formation (McGennis et al, 1977). It is not known whether childhood fears are the cause, or simply the expression of a predisposition to agoraphobia in childhood.

This would seem to indicate that a child subject to fears—hence stress—is more likely to succumb to agoraphobia in later life. The latest research confirms that this is likely.

MARITAL RELATIONSHIPS

Weekes found that of the 486 females only 51 were single, and of 42 men, 16 were single. The National Survey showed that 77.16 per cent were married or remarried, with 10.80 per cent single, 2.80 per cent divorced, 2.39 per cent separated, 6.33 per cent widowed and 0.52 per cent engaged. Since agoraphobes are generally young adults, it is logical that most surveys find the majority to be married to partners of average age.

Sexual disorder is not uncommon in agoraphobic women, particularly frigidity, but as the sexual problems can antedate the agoraphobia, no true parallel can be drawn here. Webster (1953), Roberts (1964), and Marks and Gelder (1965) respectively found 92 per cent, 53 per cent and 55 per cent of agoraphobes to be sexually maladjusted. Sexual disorder in agoraphobic women is about equal to that found in women with anxiety neurosis (Winokur and Holeman, 1963), obsessive-compulsive in-patients (Marks, 1965) and hysteria (Winokur and Leonard, 1963).

As anxiety, panic attacks and background tension form such an integral part of agoraphobia, it is not surprising that sexual problems occur. Some severe agoraphobics are known to have a satisfying sexual relationship, and as agoraphobia is often found with normal sexual enjoyment, Marks considers that sexual disorder is not a *sine qua non* for the development of agoraphobia (Marks, 1969).

The Open Door sample showed that regular sexual enjoyment and orgasm was reported in 83 per cent of the agoraphobic men, but only 60 per cent of women, which adds weight to the claim that sexual disorder is less common in agoraphobic men than women. When it does occur, it generally concerns impotence or premature ejaculation (Marks, 1969).

Although Marks claimed that the marriages of agoraphobes are generally stable, Goldstein (1970) contended that agoraphobic symptoms developed concurrently with feelings of wanting to break the marriage or of wanting to be unfaithful within marriage. This is probably correct in some cases. Agoraphobia makes a perfect trap for preventing a marriage partner from doing what he fears to do, and effectively takes the dilemma out of his/her hands. The claim that women who become agoraphobic tend to marry passive husbands has yet to be proved.

It has been found that as their wives' agoraphobia has improved, some husbands have decreased self-satisfaction, possibly because their wives are no longer totally dependent on them. A proportion of wives are unlikely to relinquish their symptoms unless the husband also receives psychiatric treatment or is included in the wife's therapy (Hafner, 1977b). In severely disabled cases, possible complementary abnormality has been found in some husbands of agoraphobes (Hafner, 1977a), and the improvement of female agoraphobes married to abnormally jealous men has resulted in increased morbidity in their husbands (Hafner, 1979). Unsatisfactory marriages are more likely to relapse after agoraphobic treatment than satisfactory ones (Milton and Hafner, 1979).

On the other hand, a Scottish survey of 30 agoraphobic housewives showed they were strikingly similar on most counts to a control group of ordinary housewives, including marital interaction (Buglass et al, 1977).

In the National Survey, 21.5 per cent felt agoraphobia was putting a considerable strain on the marital relationship. Burns and Thorpe suggest from subsequent questions that 1 in 5 of the sufferers saw their condition putting a strain on the marriage.

To summarise, although agoraphobia sufferers are subject to some sexual and marital problems, they rarely seem to have a direct bearing upon agoraphobia itself.

OCCUPATION

Job prospects are considerably affected by agoraphobia. Marks and Herst (1970) found that only 22 per cent of women were employed, and the National Survey revealed that only 28.67 per cent had a job outside the home. Weekes found that 78 per cent of her women patients were occupied at home, with 12 per cent doing part-time work, and only 10 per cent full-time work away from the home.

The National Survey showed that only a quarter of those with jobs felt that agoraphobia did little to hinder their work. Half would have changed their occupation without agoraphobia, and over 80 per cent of those not working said they would take a job outside the home if they did not have agoraphobia.

Clearly the fear of public places sets a severe handicap on those seeking employment.

PRECIPITATING FACTORS

The majority of people start to have agoraphobic symptoms after a major upset in their lives. This can be either pleasant or unpleasant, but invariably includes extra stress. (See pp. 19–21.) Weekes' patients gave the precipitating causes of their agoraphobia in the following order of frequency; physical illness (e.g. following surgery, difficult confinement, tuberculosis, infection, arthritis), domestic stress, bereavement, difficulty or pressure at work, domineering parent or parents, a parent who had had a 'nervous breakdown'—sometimes agoraphobia, unhappy parents, alcoholic parent, the sudden occurrence for the first time of agoraphobic symptoms (e.g. giddiness, panic) when out, being an only child, nervousness, illegitimacy, the Second World War, and the strain of looking after elderly parents.

Marks widens the area, including acute danger or discomfort, leaving home, engagement, marriage, pregnancy, miscarriage, or after an unpleasant scene in a shop, street or bus (Marks, 1969). Most common precipitating causes in an Irish survey were childbirth, bereavement and surgical operation (McGennis et al, 1977).

The precipitating factors for agoraphobia appear to have little relevance to the subsequent course of the disability. The main point to bear in mind is that in most cases it is a stress factor, probably pushing the person above their normal stress level.

In a few cases, phobias can start suddenly without any obvious change in the life situation of the person, although the precipitating cause may be simply 'the final straw' in a long line of nonspecific stressors in someone already liable to get the disorder.

THE SYMPTOMS OF AGORAPHOBIA

The symptoms of agoraphobia most frequently mentioned are fear of loss of control, giddiness, palpitations, difficulty in breathing, 'jelly-legs', choking feelings, sweating, headaches, stomach churning, diarrhoea, vomiting, exhaustion, panic, fear of dying, tension, loneliness, obsessive thoughts, fear of fainting, anxiety, depersonal-isation (feeling you are not really there, unreality), fear of going mad, fear of harming others, fear of illness, and being stiff with fear.

There are many other symptoms in addition to these, but in general they can be split into two distinct entities—the multiple phobias which centre on the fear of public places or going out alone, and the associated non-phobic but neurotic symptoms such as general anxiety, panic attacks, dizziness, depression, depersonal-isation and obsessions.

An Irish survey found that 76 out of 80 agoraphobes also suffered from claustrophobia and many from hypochondriacal anxiety (McGennis et al, 1977).

The diffuse anxiety which is so commonly found in agoraphobes has been borne out by various tests: psychophysiologically they have normal eyeblink conditioning, acquiring and extinguishing eyeblink conditioned responses at a normal rate (Martin et al, 1969); their skin resistance is abnormal, showing significantly in-creased spontaneous fluctuations and slowed habituation to re-peated auditory stimuli (Lader et al, 1967); and their forearm blood flow is slightly raised (Marks, 1969).

Agoraphobes are generally more fearful and depressed than other phobia sufferers and have a noticeably higher incidence of breath-ing difficulties and dizziness (Hallam and Hafner, 1978).

Even though agoraphobia and its symptoms can be regarded and treated as a clinical entity, the more diffuse varieties of agoraphobia can and do merge with anxiety states, affective disorders and some-times obsessive neuroses. These 'fringe' agoraphobia states can quite correctly be given more than one diagnostic label. It is small wonder that the diagnosis of the symptoms of agoraphobia in all its manifestations is at times both difficult and confusing.

SITUATIONS MOST FEARED BY AGORAPHOBES

Among the situations which most agoraphobes are generally cited as fearing are streets, shops, churches, cinemas, theatres, travelling in tubes, buses, trains, or any other form of travel where an easy exit is not always possible, crossing bridges and going through tunnels. Shopping is a particular nightmare, with supermarkets and department stores presenting a lot of problems. Coaches, ships and aeroplanes, and closed spaces such as lifts are also feared, although cars do not appear to present the same amount of problems.

In a survey of 900 female agoraphobes from The Open Door, 60 per cent were terrified of speaking to audiences, 50 per cent were frightened of tube trains, and 47 per cent of trains.

Gaining slightly lower percentages were theatre (39 per cent), buses (38 per cent), tunnels and heights (36 per cent), hairdresser (31 per cent), lifts (30 per cent), crowds, the dentist (28 per cent), street, open spaces (23 per cent), and parties (21 per cent). The fears were in the categories of 'frightens me even to think of it—I always avoid it' and 'terrifies me so much that every moment of my life is miserable' (Marks, 1969).

In a random sample of 100 from the National Survey, 96 per cent said that having to queue in a shop or anywhere else made them feel worse, 91 per cent said having a definite appointment had the same effect, and 89 per cent found feeling trapped at somewhere like the hairdresser's worsened their agoraphobia.

None of these situations has any particular individual significance, since the main criteria in all of them is the person's inner confidence of being able to make a quick escape. Even the presence of friends in the agoraphobe's home can be similarly terrifying if the person feels at any point that he or she has no way of getting out. Hence the feared situations are as variable as the people who have them.

SOCIAL PLOYS

The National Survey asked a random sample of 100 what factors make them feel better. 91 per cent said having a way open for a quick return home; 85 per cent, being accompanied by their marriage partner; 76 per cent, sitting near a door in a hall, restaurant, etc; 63 per cent, focusing their mind on something else; 62 per cent, taking a dog or perambulator etc on a walk, talking the problem over with a friend, and talking problems over with their doctors; 60 per cent, being accompanied by a friend; 52 per cent, talking 'sense to myself'; 36 per cent, wearing sunglasses.

TREATMENT

It would appear that agoraphobes have left no stone unturned to find a way out of their condition. The National Survey showed that 95.8 per cent of agoraphobia sufferers had seen a doctor about their condition, and over three-quarters of them had consulted a psychiatrist. 16.4 per cent had seen a religious or spiritual healer, 9.2 per cent a non-medical hypnotherapist, and 3.5 per cent a psychologist.

The vast majority (95.8 per cent) were receiving drug (tablets/medicine) treatment, with 28.9 per cent having relaxation treatment, 28.3 per cent psychotherapy/psychoanalysis, 10.7 per cent behaviour therapy, 13.5 per cent religion/faith healing and 14.9 per cent hypnotherapy.

Largely complementing this, Weekes' survey showed that 65 per cent had had treatment from one or more psychiatrists, and 30 per cent from a doctor only. Methods used included electro-convulsive therapy (ECT), psychoanalysis, narcoanalysis, hypnosis, behaviourism, insulin therapy, modified leucotomy, lysergic acid (LSD), group therapy, occupational therapy, and a great deal of drug therapy.

Other surveys add to the list, autosuggestion, deep relaxation, yoga, spiritual healing, acupuncture, psychology correspondence courses, homoeopathy, naturopathy and many other methods.

On the whole, agoraphobes are loth to seek help outside orthodox lines, although quite a few are eventually driven to this resort. The Open Door survey showed that from the time of onset of the phobia, on average it took 17 months for sufferers to go to a GP (general practitioner), 34 months to see a psychiatrist, and 57 months to go to a spiritual healer.

The success rates of various treatments do not appear to be remarkable. Of the 528 agoraphobia patients Weekes interviewed, 55 per cent said they had received no help from previous treatment, 6 per cent had been temporarily helped, and 24 per cent helped a little. Of the 15 per cent who had received positive help, Weekes found that they still needed positive support.

The results of Weekes treatment by remote direction, are remarkably good—73 per cent of patients aged 14–29 years said the results were satisfactory or good, with the oldest and hence most difficult group (50–74 years) still achieving 49 per cent for satisfactory or good progress. Good progress was interpreted as meaning agoraphobes who were able to move much more freely, and could cope if they panicked. Only 60 out of 528 sufferers claimed cure.

Very good results have been obtained from Manuel D. Zane's rather similar 'contextual therapy' with 118 (98 per cent) surveyed patients saying 'they had been helped', four (3 per cent) 'completely', and 74 (62 per cent) 'very much' (Zane, 1979).

Most benefit had been gained from treatment by the various forms of behaviour therapy, according to the National Survey. The results were still disappointing, with the behaviour therapy figure at only 31.4 per cent for those finding it very helpful. The most common treatment of tablets and medicine achieved only 16.8 per cent for those who had found it useful; a disturbing result since this is often the only treatment administered.

23.2 per cent found hypnotherapy very helpful; relaxation, 18.3 per cent; religion/faith healing, 15.5 per cent; and psychotherapy/psychoanalysis received the lowest percentage of only 14.8 per cent.

In view of this, it seems disappointing that Marks should claim that psychological treatments offer the most hope for lasting improvement for those agoraphobes without marked depression (Marks, 1978).

Marks states that with or without treatment agoraphobia tends to run a fluctuating course over years and even decades (Marks, 1969). Beech (1977) reports that once aversive responses are acquired, they are very resistant to being removed.

In The Open Door survey, only 20 per cent reported periods of complete remission once the phobias had started. Overall, 73.8 per cent of the National Survey felt they had not received adequate help for their agoraphobia. There is no particular unanimity in the claimed success for various treatments.

To summarise, it would appear from statistics that no treatment method for agoraphobia in current general use can consistently produce good results, let alone a cure. Weekes's and Zane's results are exceptional, but even here, a complete cure is rare.

ORGANIC BRAIN DYSFUNCTION (OBD) IN AGORAPHOBES

In an independent survey conducted by the author with the help of Mona Woodford and The Open Door Association, the Blythe–McGlown 'Soft Signs' OBD screening questionnaire was sent to 110 randomly selected agoraphobes. The questionnaire was probably considered a little complicated and only 21 forms were returned after two notices in The Open Door Association (TODA) newsletter.

Out of the 21 replies, 15 (71.5 per cent) scored five points or over, four (19 per cent) scored four points and two (9.5 per cent) scored three points. A score of five points is considered 'highly probable for showing the presence of OBD, and four points is considered 'highly possible'.

The results of the survey support the Blythe–McGlown findings that around 75 per cent of agoraphobia sufferers have organic brain dysfunction. (See pp. 159–60.)

REFERENCES

Agras, S., Sylvester, D. and Oliveau, D. (1969). The Epidemiology of Common Fears and Phobias. *Comprehensive Psychiatry*, 10, 2, 151.
Asso, D. and Beech, H. R. (1975). Susceptibility to the Acquisition of a Conditioned Response in Relation to the Menstrual Cycle. *Journal of Psychosomatic Research*, 19, 337.

Beech, H. R. (1977). In: The Epidemiology of Fears and Phobias, Burns, L. E. and Thorpe, G. L. *Journal of International Medical Research*, 5 (5), 3.

Bowen, R. C. and Kohout, J. (1979). The Relationship Between Agoraphobia and Primary Affective Disorders. *Canadian Journal of Psychiatry*, 24 (4), 317–322.

Buglass, D., Clarke, J., Henderson, A. S., Kreitman, N. and Presley, A. S. (1977). A Study of Agoraphobic Housewives. *Psychological Medicine*, 7 (1), 73–86.

Burns, L. E. and Thorpe, G. L. (1977a). Fears and Clinical Phobias: Epidemiological Aspects and the National Survey of Agoraphobics. *Journal of International Medical Research*, 5 (1), 132–139.

Burns, L. E. and Thorpe, G. L. (1977b). The Epidemiology of Fears and Phobias (With Particular Reference to the National Survey of Agoraphobics). *Journal of International Medical Research*, 5 (5), 1–7.

Goldstein, A. J. (1970). Case Conference: Some Aspects of Agoraphobia. *Behaviour Therapy and Experimental Psychiatry*, 1, 305.

Hafner, R. J. (1977a). The Husbands of Agoraphobic Women: Assortive Mating or Pathogenic Interaction? *British Journal of Psychiatry*, 130, 233–239.

Hafner, R. J. (1977b). The Husbands of Agoraphobic Women and Their Influence on Treatment Outcome. *British Journal of Psychiatry*, 131, 289–294.

Hafner, R. J. (1979). Agoraphobic Women Married to Abnormally Jealous Men. *British Journal of Medical Psychology*, 52 (2), 99–104.

Hallam, R. S. and Hafner, R. J. (1978). Fears of Phobic Patients: Factor Analyses of Self-report Data. *Behaviour Research and Therapy*, 16 (1), 1–6.

Harper, M. and Roth, M. (1962). Temporal Lobe Epilepsy and the Phobia-anxiety-depersonalisation Syndrome. *Comprehensive Psychiatry*, 3, 129–151.

Hollingshead, A. B. and Redlich, F. C. (1958). *Social Class and Mental Illness*. John Wiley, New York.

Kennedy, W. A. (1965). School Phobia: Rapid Treatment of 50 Cases. *Journal of Abnormal Psychology*, 70, 285.

Klein, D. F. (1964). Delineation of Two Drug-responsive Anxiety Syndromes. *Psychopharmacologia*, 5, 397–408.

Lader, M. H., Gelder, M. G. and Marks, I. M. (1967). Palmar Skin-conductance Measures as Predictors of Response to Desensitisation. *Journal of Psychosomatic Research*, 11, 283–290.

Lapouse, R. and Monk, M .A. (1959). Fears and Worries in a Representative Sample of Children. *American Journal of Orthopsychiatry*, 29, 803–818.

Lemkau, P., Tietze, C. and Cooper, M. (1942). Mental Hygiene Problems in an Urban District. *Mental Hygiene*, 26, 100.

Marks, I. M. (1965). *Patterns of Meaning in Psychiatric Patients: Semantic Differential Responses in Obsessives and Psychopaths.* Maudsley Monograph No. 13. Oxford University Press.

Marks, Isaac M. (1969). *Fears and Phobias*, Table 3.2. William Heinemann Medical Books, London.

ibid, p. 77.

ibid, p. 138.

ibid, p. 127.

ibid, p. 128.

ibid, p. 110.

ibid, Table 3.12.

ibid, p. 267.

Marks, Isaac M. (1978). *Living with Fear. Understanding and Coping with Anxiety*, p. 199. McGraw-Hill Book Company, London and New York.

Marks, I. M. and Gelder, M. G. (1965). A Controlled Retrospective Study of Behaviour Therapy in Phobic Patients. *British Journal of Psychiatry*, 111, 571–573.

Marks, I. M. and Gelder, M. G. (1969). In: *Fears and Phobias*, p. 166. Marks, I. M. William Heinemann Medical Books, London.

Marks, I. M. and Herst, E. R. (1969). A Survey of 1,200 Agoraphobics in Britain. *Social Psychiatry*, 5, 16.

Martin, I., Marks, I. M. and Gelder, M. G. (1969). Conditioned Eyelid Responses in Phobic Patients. *Behaviour Research and Therapy*, 7.

McGennis, A., Hartman, M. and Nolan, G. (1977). The Role of a Self-help Association in Agoraphobia: One Year's Experience with 'Out and About'. *Irish Medical Journal*, 70 (1), 10–13.

Milton, F. and Hafner, R. J. (1979). The Outcome of Behavior Therapy for Agoraphobia in Relation to Marital Adjustment. *Archives of General Psychiatry*, 36 (7), 807–811.

Prince, M. and Putnam, J. J. (1912). Clinical Study of a Case of Phobia: A Symposium. *Journal of Abnormal and Social Psychology*, 7, 259–303.

Roberts, A. H. (1964). Housebound Housewives—A Follow-up Study of a Phobic Anxiety State. *British Journal of Psychiatry*, 110, 191–197.

Roth, M. (1959). The Phobic-anxiety-depersonalisation Syndrome. *Proceedings of the Royal Society of Medicine*, 52 (8), 587.

Rutter, M., Tizard, J. and Whitmore, K. (1968). Chapter 12 in *Education, Health and Behaviour*. Longman, London.

Snaith, R. P. (1968). A Clinical Investigation of Phobias. *British Journal of Psychiatry*, 114, 673–698.

Terhune, W. (1949). The Phobic Syndrome: A Study of 86 Patients with Phobic Reactions. *Archives of Neurological Psychiatry*, 62, 162–172.

Webster, A. S. (1953). The Development of Phobias in Married Women. *Psychology Monograph*, 67, No. 367.

Weekes, Claire (1973). A Practical Treatment of Agoraphobia. *British Medical Journal*, 2, 469–471.

Wilson, G. D. (1967). Social Desirability and Sex Differences in Expressed Fear. *Behaviour Research and Therapy*, 5, 136–137.

Winokur, G. and Holeman, E. (1963). Chronic Anxiety Neurosis: Clinical and Sexual Aspects. *Acta Psychiatrica Scandinavica*, 39, 384–412.

Winokur, G. and Leonard, C. (1963). Sexual Life in Patients with Hysteria. *Diseases of the Nervous System*, 24, 1–7.

Zane, Manuel D. (1979). Treatment Strategies and Programs. Excerpt from *Cognitive Behaviour Therapy Newsletter*, 2, No. 1, October.

Select Bibliography

Additional to main text references

Basker, M. A. (1979). A Hypnobehavioural Method of Treating Agoraphobia by the Clenched Fist Method of Calvert Stein. *Australian Journal of Clinical and Experimental Hypnosis*, 7 (1), 27–34.

Blythe, P. and McGlown, D. J. (1981). Minimal Brain Dysfunction and Organic Brain Dysfunction. Läkartidningen, *Journal of the Swedish Medical Association*, 78, 45–48.

Butler, Pamela E. (1975). The Treatment of Severe Agoraphobia employing Induced Anger as an Anxiety Inhibitor: A Case Study. *Journal of Behavior Therapy and Experimental Psychiatry*, 6 (4), 327–329.

Chiari, Gabriele and Mosticoni, Roberto (1979). The Treatment of Agoraphobia with Biofeedback and Systematic Desensitisation. *Journal of Behaviour Therapy and Experimental Psychiatry*, 10 (2), 109–113.

Colgan, M. (1979). Use of Biofeedback in Systematic Desensitization of Phobias. *NZ Nursing Forum—Journal of the Nurses Society of New Zealand*, 7 (2), 4–7.

Deiker, T. E. and Pollock, D. H. (1975). Integration of Hypnotic and Systematic Desensitization Techniques in the Treatment of Phobias: a Case Report. *American Journal of Clinical Hypnosis*, 17 (3), 170–174.

Emmelkamp, P. M. G. and Wessels, H. (1975). Flooding in Imagination versus Flooding In Vivo: a Comparison with Agoraphobics. *Behaviour Research and Therapy*, 13 (1), 7–15.

Emmelkamp, P. M. G., Kuipers, A. C. M. and Eggeraat, J. B. (1978). Cognitive Modification Versus Prolonged Exposure In Vivo: A Comparison with Agoraphobics as Subjects. *Behaviour Research and Therapy*, 16 (1), 33–41.

Emmelkamp, P. M. G. and Kuipers, A. C. M. (1979). Agoraphobia: A Follow-up Study Four Years after Treatment. *British Journal of Psychiatry*, 134, 352–355.

Frampton, Muriel (1974). *Overcoming Agoraphobia: Coping with the World Outside*. Thorsons, Wellingborough.

Frankel, F. H. and Orne, M. T. (1976). Hypnotizability and Phobic Behavior. *Archives of General Psychiatry*, 33 (10), 1259–1261.

Gelder, M. G. (1979). Behavioural Treatment for Psychiatric Disorders in General Practice: Preliminary Communication. *Journal of the Royal Society of Medicine*, 72 (6), 421–424.

Goldstein, Alan J. and Chambless, Dianne L. (1978). A Reanalysis of Agoraphobia. *Behavior Therapy*, 9 (1), 47–59.

Gruenewald, D. (1971). Agoraphobia: a Case Study in Hypnotherapy. *International Journal of Clinical and Experimental Hypnosis*, 19 (1), 10–20.

Klein, D. F., Zitrin, C. M. and Woerner, M. G. (1977). Imipramine and Phobia. *Psychopharmacology Bulletin*, 13 (2), 24–27.

Lee, I. and Tyrer, P. (1980). Responses of Chronic Agoraphobics to Subliminal and Supraliminal Phobic Motion Pictures. *Journal of Nervous and Mental Disease*, 168 (1), 34–40.

Lyle, Ronald C. (1980). *Manual for the Treatment of Agoraphobia by Behavioural Methods*. Stobhill General Hospital, Glasgow.

Mann, H. B. and Greenspan, S. I. (1976). The Identification and Treatment of Adult Brain Dysfunction. *American Journal of Psychiatry*, 133 (9), 1013–1017.

Mathews, A. (1977). Recent Developments in the Treatment of Agoraphobia. *Behavioural Analysis and Modification*, 2 (1), 64–75.

Munby, M. and Johnston, D. W. (1980). Agoraphobia: The Long-term Follow-up of Behavioural Treatment. *British Journal of Psychiatry*, 137 (5), 418–427.

Orwin, A., le Boeuf, A., Dovey, J. and James, S. (1975). A Comparative Trial of Exposure and Respiratory Relief Therapies. *Behaviour Research and Therapy*, 13 (4), 205–214.

Popler, Kenneth (1977). Agoraphobia: Indications for the Application of the Multimodal Behavioral Conceptualization. *Journal of Nervous and Mental Disease*, 164 (2), 97–101.

Rohs, R. G. and Noyes, R. Jr. (1978). Agoraphobia: Newer Treatment Approaches. *Journal of Nervous and Mental Disease*, 166 (10), 701–8.

Ross, J. (1980). The Use of Former Phobics in the Treatment of Phobias. *American Journal of Psychiatry*, 137 (6), 715–717.

Sheehan, D. V., Ballenger, J. and Jacobsen, G. (1980). Treatment of Endogenous Anxiety with Phobic, Hysterical and Hypochondriacal Symptoms. *Archives of General Psychiatry*, 37 (1), 51–59.

Stern, Richard (1978). *Behavioural Techniques: A Therapist's Manual*. Academic Press, New York.

Teasdale, J. D., Walsh, P. A., Lancashire, M. and Mathews, A. M. (1977). Group Exposure for Agoraphobics: A Replication Study. *British Journal of Psychiatry*, 130, 186–193.

Weekes, Claire (1972). *Peace from Nervous Suffering*. Angus and Robertson, London.

Weekes, Claire (1976). *Simple, Effective Treatment of Agoraphobia*. Hawthorn Books, New York.

Weekes, Claire (1979). *Simple, Effective Treatment of Agoraphobia*. Bantam paperback, London.

Zane, M. D. (1978). Contextual Analysis and Treatment of Phobic Behaviour as it Changes. *American Journal of Psychotherapy*, 32 (3), 338–356.

Zitrin, C. M., Klein, D. F. and Woerner, M. G. (1978). Behavior Therapy, Supportive Psychotherapy, Imipramine, and Phobias. *Archives of General Psychiatry*, 35 (3), 307–316.

Zitrin, C. M., Klein, D. F. and Woerner, M. G. (1980). Treatment of Agoraphobia with Group Exposure In Vivo and Imipramine. *Archives of General Psychiatry*, 37 (1), 63–72.

Useful Addresses in the United Kingdom

A self-addressed stamped envelope should be sent with all enquiries.

Courses and clinics for agoraphobes are run occasionally by some of the larger hospitals throughout the UK and enquiries must be made through general practitioners.

Local Citizens' Advice Bureaux may supply phobic addresses and help can also be obtained through local Samaritan branches. Both can be located through the telephone directory.

MIND (National Association for Mental Health)
22 Harley Street
London W1N 2ED

Phobic Societies (United Kingdom and Republic of Ireland)

Mona Woodford
National Organiser, The Open Door Association
447 Pensby Road
Heswall, Wirral
Merseyside L61 9PQ

Katherine Fisher
President, The Phobics Society
4 Cheltenham Road
Chorlton-cum-Hardy
Manchester M21 1QN

Phobias Confidential
1 Clovelly Road
Ealing, London W5 5HF

Tony Elliott
Founder President, Nottingham and County Phobic Association
1 Oban Road
Chilwell, Nottingham

Pam Moscrop
Horizon
244 Whickham View
Denton Burn
Newcastle-upon-Tyne

Morny Murrihy
Out and About Association
St Johns House, Seafield Road
Clontarf, Dublin 3

Acupuncture

British Medical Acupuncture Society
21 Aigburth Drive
Sefton Park
Liverpool L17 4JQ

British Acupuncture Association and Register
Harvester House, 37 Peter Street
Manchester M2 5QD
London Office:
34 Alderney Street
London SW1V 4EU

Alexander Technique

Society of Teachers of Alexander Technique
3b Albert Court
Kensington Gore
London SW7

Biofeedback

Classes and courses are run by:
C. Maxwell Cade
c/o Audio Limited
26 Wendell Road
London W12 9RT

The Wreakin Trust
Bowler House, Bridstow
Ross-on-Wye
Herefordshire

Chiropractic

British Chiropractors' Association
5 First Avenue
Chelmsford
Essex CM1 1RA

Claire Weekes' cassettes and records available from:
16 Rivermead Court
Ranelagh Gardens
London SW6 3RT

also stocked by The Open Door Association.

Co-counselling

For details on Co-counselling International contact:
London Co-counsellors
c/o Anne Dickson
83 Fordwych Road
London NW2 3TL

Herbalism

John D. Hyde FNIMH
President, National Institute of Medical Herbalists
68 London Road
Leicester LE2 0OD

Homoeopathy

Maureen Munday
General Secretary, The British Homoeopathic Association
27a Devonshire Street
London W1N 1RJ

Hypnotism and Psychotherapy

British Society for Medical and Dental Hypnosis
10 Chillerton Road
London SW17 9BG

Association of Hypnotists and Psychotherapists
168 Brownside Road
Worsthorne, Burnley
Lancashire BB10 3JW

Naturopathy and Osteopathy

British Naturopathic and Osteopathic Association
Frazer House
6 Netherhall Gardens
London NW3 5RR

The General Council and Register of Osteopaths
16 Buckingham Gate
London SW1E 6LB

Yoga

Howard Kent
Director, The Yoga for Health Foundation
Ickwell Bury, Biggleswade
Bedfordshire SG18 9EF

Useful Addresses in the United States of America

Manuel D. Zane MD
The Phobia Clinic
White Plains Hospital
Davis Avenue, White Plains
New York 10601

Charlotte M. Zitrin MD
Director, The Phobia Clinic
Long Island Jewish-Hillside Medical Center
PO Box 38, Glen Oaks
New York 11004

The Behavior Therapy Center of New York
115 East 87th Street
New York
New York 10028

For list of Terrap centres and information sheet write to:

Terrap-Menlo Park
1010 Dyle Street
Menlo Park
California 94025

A general list of treatment facilities for agoraphobes can be ordered from:

Temple University
Agoraphobia Program
3401 North Broad Street
Philadelphia
Pennsylvania 19140

Behaviour Therapists are listed with:

The Association for Advancement of Behavior Therapy
420 Lexington Avenue
New York
New York 10017

Rolfing

Rolf Institute
PO Box 1868
Boulder
Colorado 80306

Organic Brain Dysfunction Therapy Centres in England and Sweden

The Institute for Neuro-Physiological Psychology
Warwick House
4 Stanley Place
Chester
Cheshire

J. P. Noble
10 Branch Road
Park Street
St Albans
Herefordshire AL2 2LU

The Swedish Institute for Neuro-Physiological Psychology
Berzeliigatan 19 IV
412 53
Gothenburg
Sweden

Index